"Whether you are beginning a career in sales
or have been at it a few years,
this is a book for you."

-Prospero, Amazon 5-Star Review

"...Rugg is a mine of SF-related information."

-Tomb Owler, Amazon 5-Star Review

Rugg's Handbook of

Sales and Science Fiction

Rugg's Handbook of

Sales
and
Science Fiction

Tips, Tricks and Lessons
From the Genre of Science Fiction
To Help You Achieve a
Sales Career that is
Out Of This World!

Raymond Rugg

International Standard Book Number:

ISBN-13:
978-1483910161

ISBN-10:
1483910164

As ever, for IAK

Contents

Introduction   vii
In the beginning
Sales philosophy
What you'll find in the handbook
Notes

Acknowledgements   xiii

Lessons
1. *Dune*, novel   2
2. *Doctor Who: Asylum of the Daleks*, television series episode   4
3. *Girl Genius*, web comic   6
4. *Have You Heard the One...?*, short story   8
5. *War of the Worlds*, radio play adaptation   10
6. *Planet of the Apes*, movie   12
7. *If This Goes On---*, novelette   14
8. *The Invisible Man*, novel   16
9. *Star Wars*, movie trilogy   18
10. *2001: A Space Odyssey*, movie   20
11. *The Man Who Sold the Moon*, novelette   22
12. *Star Trek*, movie   24
13. *Star Trek*, novelization   26
14. Heinlein's first sale, industry anecdote   28
15. *A Plague of Demons*, novel   30
16. *Valor's Choice*, novel   32
17. *Inception*, movie   34
18. *Firefly*, television series   36
19. *The Matrix*, movie   38
20. Genre cover art, industry anecdote   40
21. The self-promotion of Isaac Asimov, industry anecdote   42
22. *Off Armaggedon Reef*, novel   44
23. *Fahrenheit 451*, novel   46
24. *The Mote in God's Eye*, novel   48
25. *Absolution Gap*, novel   50

26. The Terminator, movie   52
27. *Whose Face This Is, I Do Not Know,* short story   54
28. *The Majipoor Chronicles,* short story collection   56
29. Astounding Science Fiction November 1949,
                             industry anecdote   58
30. *Alien,* movie, novelization   60
31. The careers of William Shatner
                  and Leonard Nimoy, industry anecdote   62
32. *Perhaps to Dream,* short story   66
33. *Little Brother,* novel   68
34. *Star Wars Episode I: The Phantom Menace,* movie   70
35. Sturgeon's Law, industry anecdote   72
36. The Career of James Gunn, industry anecdote   74
37. *Bicentennial Man,* novelette   76
38. *The Vor Game,* novel   78
39. Clarke's Third Law, industry anecdote   80
40. *Blade Runner,* movie   82
41. *The Science of Science-Fiction Writing,* non-fiction book   84
42. *The Hitchhiker's Guide to the Galaxy,* novel   86

Index   89

Further Info   95

Introduction

In the beginning

I've been a science fiction fan for nearly as long as I've been able to read. On second thought, I've been a science fiction fan for *longer* than I've been able to read; I can recall being fascinated by the Disney movie version of Jules Verne's *20,000 Leagues Under the Sea* sometime before I was old enough for elementary school.

I've been in sales for almost as long. As a youngster, I set up shop on the side of the road outside of town and flagged down passing motorists in order to sell them tickets to the regional Boy Scout Jamboree. It sounds crazy, and I'd have a heart attack if one of my kids were doing the same today. But on the other hand, I *did* win the troop prize for selling the most tickets. I sold as many tickets on my own as the entire rest of the troop sold all together. It's an achievement that I'm still proud of today, some decades after the fact. (I mean, here I am, bragging about it after all this time, so it must have made some sort of impact on me.)

In the many years since, I've held several jobs, including stints in journalism, public relations, and teaching. But it's the sales jobs that keep drawing me back, whether it's advertising, retail, telemarketing, or door-to-door pounding-the-pavement sales. It's because sales is one of the only gigs in which the more success you have, the more money you make. It's more results-oriented than process-oriented. Of course, this isn't a universal statement; but for the most part, if you earn a commission, you make *more money* when you sell *more product* (or service). You also make less money when you fail to sell, but that's all part-and-parcel of the thrill of the sales life.

And like most people, I'd like to be better at what I do. Particularly when, as in sales, how good you are can be directly proportional to how much you make. So I buy the sales books, looking for ways to improve my sales skills. I read the business strategy books, I read the management biographies. I read these books in order to learn new sales philosophies, and I read these books to remind me of the sales strategies and methods that I already know, but may have been neglecting. I read them for inspiration. And in between, I also watch and read science fiction. A lot of sci-fi and speculative fiction. (Sci-fi, science fiction, spec fic, fantasy... I'll go into a deeper discussion of terminology and analysis of this further along.)

But one day, as I was re-reading Frank Herbert's *Dune*, a certain situation struck me as familiar... not familiar from my reading of science fiction for entertainment, but familiar from my day-to-day sales life. I jotted it down in a notebook. After that, I began to see lessons for my sales career in a lot of different science fiction, and not just in books, but also in films, television shows, even in the behind-the-scenes stories and legends of the SF genre. I began to blog about it, and then I began to collect these lessons in book form. And the lesson that began it all, from Herbert's *Dune*, became Lesson 1 of my handbook of sales and science fiction.

Because these are lessons gathered over the years, and from across the spectrum of the genre, I encourage you to read this book more as a collection of distinct and individual entries than as one flowing piece of work. Some of the entries may seem contradictory; different lessons may apply to different sales situations. Some of the lessons may not be the same as the ones that you might draw from the stories; these are the lessons that *I* have derived from my own sales experiences and my own reading or viewing of the science fiction. Pick and choose, feel free to disagree, and draw your own conclusions; the point of this book is to show you how *I* use science fiction to help me in my sales career, and to get you started on the path toward drawing your own lessons from the genre.

And while we're on the subject, I'll tell you this up front. To me, Science Fiction is fun. And sales is fun. So I want a book called *Sales and Science Fiction* to be fun. Fun-fun. Fun-squared. You're going to run into slang, colloquialisms, and even (gasp!) *incomplete sentences*. You'll encounter irreverence, skepticism, and self-indulgent comments. I had fun writing this book, and I'd like you to have fun reading it. (If you do, I'd like to hear about it. Drop me a note at **salesandscifi@gmail.com**. And oh, what the heck; drop me a note even if you don't have fun, but do have something constructive to add to the conversation.) The point is, this isn't a management whitepaper. It's me sharing my passion with you. It is what it is.

Sales philosophy

In my sales career, I have done door-to-door, I've done telemarketing, I've done retail, I've done membership sales, I've done inside sales, outside sales, I've done B2B and I've done B2C. I've done a lot of sales. And in every sales job I've ever had, my goal has been to make my customers' and clients' lives better, and to be appropriately compensated financially for doing so.

I'm not out to be the guy who does the sales equivalent of slash-and-burn. I'm out to help clients. Sometimes that means that my product isn't the best fit for the client. So I might not get a sale in that instance; that's life. With luck (and a friendly, respectful reminder now and then), the client will remember this honesty and believe me when the time comes that I can tell them that my product really is the best fit for what they need.

Sometimes what is best for the client isn't what the client thinks is best. The client isn't really always right. But if they insist on their own way, even after you explain why a different way is better, then you have to respect their decision. Whoever is putting up the cash has the final say. It's like in the newspaper biz. (Newspapers, remember those? Big sheets of thin paper with news and articles and advertisements on them?) If a reporter writes an article about a business, the business might have some input, but ultimately, no control over what is printed. On the other hand, if the business takes out an ad, they get to dictate exactly what goes into that space (assuming it's legal, of course).

And in exchange for my hard work to provide solutions to clients' problems, I expect adequate and appropriate pay. I'll admit that there have been times in the past when I've tried to sell on price, or sweeten a sales deal at the expense of my own bottom line. But I've come to realize that whatever value you place on your product or service becomes the automatic maximum value that anyone will place on it. If you discount your price, then even your good friends and clients will feel that your service is *worth* only that amount. In the end, you do no one-- not yourself, not your clients, and not your industry-- any favors by accepting less than what you are really worth, just in order to make a sale.

So that's the underlying thought behind the lessons in this book: Do what's best for the clients, and get paid fairly for doing so.

What you'll find in the handbook

In this book, I offer up 42 entries, 42 lessons derived from stories or situations in the SF genre. Each entry comprises the following:

> **The Sci-Fi:** The source material
> **The Sci-Fi Sitch:** The situation; the circumstances in a nutshell
> **The Sales Sitch:** How the Sci-Fi sitch relates to a sales situation
> **The Sales and Sci-Fi Lesson:** The lesson presented in one or two sentences
> **The Sci-Fi Skinny:** The framework or context of the source material, background info, or some interesting trivia.

Following the Lessons section, there is an Index and there is a Further Info list. The entries in this book are not presented in a particular order or with an over-arching theme, with the exception of the first and last entries. The first, *Dune*, leads off the list due to the fact that this was the sales lesson that started the entire project. The last, Number 42, from *The Hitchhiker's Guide to the Galaxy*, closes out the list because this lesson helped me to decide on how many lessons should be included in the collection. If you don't get the reference right off the bat, don't worry; you'll understand when you get to that lesson.

And finally… **!Spoiler Alert!** These entries are presented with the assumption that the reader is at least somewhat familiar with the plots of the stories. If you haven't read the book or seen the movie being discussed, and don't want to know what happens in the story, DON'T READ THE ENTRY! In many cases, the entry provides a plot summary in order to tie the science fiction to the sales lesson. I really don't want to ruin anyone's enjoyment of reading or watching science fiction, so please consider this to be fair warning.

And now, please feel free to skip on over to the Lessons! The final notes that follow here in the introduction are more along the lines of minutia that's mostly of interest only to hardcore geeks and copy editors. (Yes, I'm guilty on both counts.)

Notes:

In this book, I have used several terms interchangeably. In my literary travels, I have seen the word 'science fiction' presented as science fiction, Science Fiction, Science fiction, Science-Fiction, Science-fiction, and science-fiction. There is the shortened slang term, derived from old library labeling, of Sci-Fi, sci-fi, or Sci-fi. It's sometimes shortened all the way down to SF, which can also stand for speculative fiction (which is also sometimes presented as Speculative Fiction, Speculative fiction, Speculative-Fiction, speculative-fiction, Speculative-fiction, spec-fic, Spec-Fic, or Spec-fic.) I'm sure you've already spotted the potential for hours of etymological fun for the whole family.

While I use several of the variations in this handbook, what you'll see most often is Science Fiction as the long term and Sci-Fi as the short term. I know that some purists balk at this nickname for the genre, but I don't mind it. And since it's my book, it's my preferences we'll be going with.

And in my book, or in this one, at least, we're drawing specifically from Science Fiction. The Sales and Fantasy sales lessons will be coming along in the second book. "But wait," cry readers who aren't hip to the subtleties of the genre, "what's the difference between the two, between Science Fiction and Fantasy?"

Heh. I'm glad you asked!
I consider Science Fiction to be fiction that has some sort of fantastic element that can be explained as falling under the laws of nature, natural laws that may or may not be understood by us at this point in our technological progress. This would, then, include such stories as space travel and contact with aliens, stories of robots and androids, time-travel by way of scientific technology, and so on.

Fantasy, on the other hand, includes a fantastic element of *super*natural origin. First and foremost, this includes magic. It also includes supernatural horror, such as vampires, werewolves, ghosts and the like. Dragons, dwarfs, elves, sorcery and all that jazz.

Sometimes, Science Fiction and Fantasy can blend into one another. Anne McCaffrey's Dragonriders books come across as great fantasy, but even from the very beginning, she made it clear that Pern was a colonized planet and that the threat of Thread came from a neighboring astronomical body. Strictly speaking, the Pern books would be Sci-Fi, but I prefer to read them as Fantasy, at least the ones that are earlier in the series. Stephen King's *11/22/63* is a time-travel story, which *could* fit into the Science Fiction category, but to me has supernatural-ish elements, and I have classified it as Fantasy. You get the idea. There's a lot of gray area in the borderlands between Sci-Fi and Fantasy.

As far as the terms Speculative Fiction and Spec-Fic go, I use this label as an umbrella term for both Science Fiction and Fantasy. It's a handy way to lump the sub-genres into one big genre without having to make those pesky differentiations between them. Spec-Fic is also a convenient label for Alternate History stories; this sub-genre doesn't seem to me to fit into either Science Fiction or Fantasy, yet obviously doesn't fit well into your normal Historical Fiction category.

All of this, of course, is my own personal method of pigeon-holing the stuff that I like to read and to watch. It's a layman's view, a fanboy's take on the genre. For a true academic discussion of the issue, I respectfully point you toward the writings of James Gunn. If you are really interested in the literary taxonomy of the genre, please refer to *Toward a Definition of Science Fiction,* which is Chapter 13 of his *The Science of Science-Fiction Writing.* And finally, a brief word on the Index and Further Info list that follow the lessons. The Index is pretty straight-forward; I've included most of the creative personalities and their works, as well as organizations, awards and publications, as a way for the reader to find these entries in the body of the book. I have not included fictional personalities, places, etc. in the Index; I wanted to, but then the Index threatened to become larger than the book itself, so if you want to track down characters and storylines and such-all, you'll have to do the footwork yourself.

The Further Info list also wanted to grow to a size of farcical proportions, so it had to be pruned to entries on the primary personalities and the like, the ones with a *direct* impact on the sales lessons. For the most part, they will lead you to the official websites of the entry, or at least a fairly definitive fan site. And if you're reading this book, I figure you can handle Google, or any other search engine of your choice, well enough to find whatever you're looking for. This list is just intended to be a convenient starting point for anyone who wants to poke around a little bit more.

Okay, thanks for reading. Now on to business!

Acknowledgements

On the Sci-Fi side, many thanks go out to all the industry folk that took the time to chat with me about their own work and the works of others, with special thanks to Cat Rambo and Alistair Reynolds. Extra-special thanks to Chris McKitterick of the Center for the Study of Science Fiction, and thanks without end to James Gunn of the CSSF-- author, editor, scholar, teacher of SF and SFWA Grand Master — for his comments and communications.

On the sales side, I've worked with quite a few sales managers and old sales pros throughout the years, and I like to think that I learned something from each of them. Many will recognize their teachings in this book. But I've also learned a lot from people who didn't have the word "sales" anywhere in their title, yet sales made up an important part of what they did, day in and day out. When you get down to it, life is sales. So a sincere thanks goes out to all of these folks, the ones in sales and the ones in life. You know who you are.

On the home front, thanks to my folks and my brothers: it was an awfully SF-friendly environment at the Rugg Ranch (and still is!) Thanks, Dad.

And finally, there's no way this could ever have been conceived or accomplished without the constant support of my wife and daughters. Editors, beta-readers, and my connection to the contemporary worlds of Speculative Fiction. My life is a fanboy's dream come true, all thanks to my three girls. To lift a phrase, they are my Ideal Readers.

The Lessons

Lesson 1

The Sci-Fi: *Dune.* **Novel by Frank Herbert.**

The Sci-Fi Sitch: In a far-distant future of inter-stellar economic and royal feudalism, political forces maneuver House Atreides to be conquered by the rival House Harkonnen. Young Paul Atreides, son of the Duke, survives the attack, and goes on to join with the Fremen peoples of the planet Arrakis- also known as Dune- to wage and win a religious guerrilla jihad against the Harkonnens and the empire.

Early in the novel, before the trap against the Atreides has been sprung, Paul is training with his tutor/mentor/man-at-arms, the warrior Gurney Halleck, and doing poorly in his fencing exercises. He states that he "isn't in the mood" for swordplay. Halleck responds by growling that moods are for other activities, such as music or lovemaking, but not for fighting, and proceeds to attack Paul in what seems to be an earnest attempt to injure, or even kill the boy. Surprised and concerned for his life, Paul Atreides defends himself, calling upon his martial training and skills to fend Halleck off, until the trainer is satisfied that the boy has learned his lesson and has sufficiently overcome his 'not being in the mood to fight.'

The Sales Sitch: You'll notice that Gurney Halleck didn't include 'Sales' in his list of activities for which 'being in the mood' is a requisite. The harsh reality is that nobody-- not your manager, not your clients, and not anyone else in the universe-- much cares whether you're in the mood for sales. (Although, come to think of it, it might please your competitors.) Whether you're happy, sad, fired up, depressed, sleepy, energized or whatever, your prospects still need to be prospected, your clients still need to be serviced, and your product still needs to be sold.

Do what it takes to fix the situation. Call on one of your better and more satisfied customers in order to give yourself an ego boost. Crunch some numbers and set a short-term target or goal. Do *something* to get yourself back to work.

The Sales and Sci-Fi Lesson: You can wait until you're in the mood in order to participate in some activities. But for fighting-- and sales-- you need to get out there and do what needs to be done, and let the 'mood' follow as it will.

The Sci-Fi Skinny: *Dune* (Frank Herbert, American author, 1920-1986) was published in 1965, and this novel routinely ranks near or at the top of most lists of the best science fiction books. It won both the Nebula and Hugo awards, and was the first of some six Dune novels by Herbert. Authors Kevin J. Anderson and Brian Herbert (Frank Herbert's son) have written prequels and sequels to Frank Herbert's Dune books, based on Frank Herbert's unpublished notes. So far, the original *Dune* has been presented as both a major motion picture and a Sci-Fi (now Syfy) Channel mini-series, among other re-presentations of the story, and there seems to be perpetual movie industry talk of further film versions of the novel.

Lesson 2

The Sci-Fi: *Doctor Who; Asylum of the Daleks.* **Season 7, Episode 1 of the (revived) television show** *Doctor Who.* **Directed by Nick Hurran and written by Steven Moffat.**

The Sci-Fi Sitch: In the first episode of season 7 of *Doctor Who*, the inimitable Time Lord (in his 11th incarnation, portrayed by Matt Smith) has been kidnapped by the Dalek Parliament. (The Daleks being, as the BBC puts it, "his oldest foe.") They want him to travel down to a planet where they have quarantined those members of their race who are considered to be too crazy and destructive even for Dalek society. The Doctor and companions Amy and Rory Pond are beamed down to this 'Asylum of the Daleks,' and well, no, hilarity does not ensue, but plenty of scary and emotional scenes are experienced by all.

The Sales Sitch: Do you know how many times the Doctor has defeated the Daleks? Neither did I. But when I saw this episode, I figured it had to be up there in the dozens. (In fact, the UK's *Guardian*, as of this particular episode, pegged it at 34 storylines involving the Daleks.) Didn't he even destroy them *all* in the Last Great Time War? (Well, yes, but no. You know, wibbly-wobbly, timey-whimey.) But they just. Keep. Coming. Back. New season, new battle with the Daleks.

And that's the sales lesson to be drawn from this. Your toughest competitors are always out there in the shadows, waiting to take advantage at any time. There is a sales saying to the effect that the day you sign a client is the day you start losing them. That's the flip-side to the lesson of the Daleks. The day you beat your 'oldest foe' is the day that that foe begins another campaign that will be the end of you, or will take the client away from you, if you're not careful.

The Sales and Sci-Fi Lesson: Don't ever count your competitor out of the running, because they will always come back. The best you can do is to beat them for now- beat them this season, beat them this episode, beat them this sales cycle.

The Sci-Fi Skinny: *Doctor Who* is a BBC television series about a Time Lord, an alien adventurer through time and space in his TARDIS, which looks on the outside like a British police box and is, famously, bigger on the inside. Guinness World Records pegs Doctor Who as the World's Most Successful Sci-Fi series, as well as being the Longest Running Sci-Fi series. And the related media are beyond number, from books to radio shows to comics and on to infinity. As far as the television show itself, the original ran from 1963 to 1989. There was a sputtering attempt to re-launch it in 1996, and then in 2005, Doctor Who returned to television with a vengeance, and has been going strong ever since, including a big 50th anniversary bash in 2013.

Lesson 3

The Sci-Fi: *Girl Genius*. **Web comic by Phil and Kaja Foglio.**

The Sci-Fi Sitch: The setting of *Girl Genius* is steampunk-flavored Europe, 1800's-ish or so. Mad science is the rule of the day, with those who have the innate talent, or spark, doing all sorts of crazy stuff, like building robots (clanks) and artificial humanoids (constructs), re-animating the dead, creating sentient castles, and all that kind of thing. The continental power is in the person of Baron Wulfenbach, an iron-handed tyrant ruling from his dirigible castle. The story begins some years following the defeat of an alien enemy of humanity, the Other, by the Baron and his allies/rivals, the Heterodyne Brothers. In this gaslamp adventure, when the mad science talent blooms in one of the sparks, it is a breakthrough (often traumatic), a sudden burst of ability or inclination, and Wulfenbach strives to gather these talents up to work for him (willingly or not).

The Sales Sitch: There seems to be a sort of breakthrough that can occur in sales, the same kind of breakthrough that is experienced by the 'sparks' of Girl Genius. I have observed it in a number of different sales situations, and I have heard the concept from a number of different and disparate sales veterans and managers (expressed in different terms, but with the same underlying theme).

Sales sparks often experience breakthroughs in the *third* selling cycle of their particular field or industry. Some poor sales slob will start a job and be plugging away, maybe just making quota, maybe just *not* making quota, banging his or her head against the wall, getting frustrated and questioning the wisdom of getting into this particular line. And then, if they can hang on through the third sales cycle, all of a sudden everything seems to click. Presentations go well, prospects turn into clients, existing clients upgrade their orders, and other prospects actually come around seeking the sales rep out. For something like advertising sales in a daily or weekly publication, this breakthrough might happen after three months in. For a product with a longer sales cycle, the spark might have to stick with it for three quarters in order to experience this burst of success. And for others it may mean three years into the job, for example if the rep is involved in seasonal sales (selling to summer or winter resorts, sales related to a particular holiday or sport) or yearly sales (educational markets tied to the school year).

Of course, there are sales reps who jump into a job like a duck jumps into water. They might be successful at it from day one. On the flip side, there are those who jump into it like an anvil jumps into water... they sink, and nothing will ever, ever make them float. But sometimes, *sometimes*, if a rep will struggle and struggle, and then, BAM, all of a sudden, in the third sales cycle, they come into their own.

The Sales and Sci-Fi Lesson: Keep on plugging away; even if things are going badly, it might be that you are a sales spark just about to blossom into some mad sales success. Look for a breakthrough after the third sales cycle.

The Sci-Fi Skinny: I have used the *Omnibus Volume One: Agatha Awakens* hardback collection of Girl Genius as a reference for this sales lesson. Girl Genius is a web comic by the unparalleled husband-wife team of Phil and Kaja Foglio. The comic posts to the web on Mondays, Wednesdays and Fridays, and in addition to being what their publisher, TOR books, calls "the acclaimed, multiple-Hugo Award-winning steampunk fantasy adventure," the storyline is also available in novel form. And yes, there are fantasy elements to Girl Genius, but it is a story about Mad Science, and therefore fits my requirements for Sci-Fi.

Lesson 4

The Sci-Fi: *Have You Heard the One...?* **Short story by Spider Robinson.**

The Sci-Fi Sitch: At Callahan's famous Crosstime Saloon, it's Wednesday night. That is to say, Tall Tales Night. The festivities are interrupted by the arrival of a jolly, fascinating, wonderful fellow who turns out to be a traveling salesman. His name is Al Phee, and he says he's from outer space and wants to sell the folks at the tavern some magic jewels in exchange for all of their pennies. (Trust me, it holds together in Robinson's story much better than in my summary.) Well, it turns out good ol' Al is actually living up to, that is, *down* to, the worst reputation of sales, and is trying to con Callahan and the saloon's clientele, to pull a fast one over on them.

The Sales Sitch: As a sales person, you should cringe when you read about the Traveling Salesman archetype, the fast-talking scoundrel out to take financial advantage of everyone he encounters. And you should realize that this is the mental image that a large portion of the population, i.e., your clients and prospects, still possess in that brain slot marked 'salesman'. As noted in Blair Singer's book, *Sales Dogs*, many people rank the occupation of 'sales' just below that of 'sewage technician'. (When I told my brother this, he laughed. He's a sewage technician. (Really.)) You have to keep in mind that no matter how sincere you are, no matter how helpful, no matter how much you really and truly care about your clients' best interests, you are fighting an uphill public relations battle against the stereotype of the selfish, sleazy salesman. Only time and experience with you will wipe the slate clean and let people know you for the great guy or gal that you really are.

The Sales and Sci-Fi Lesson: Society has an ingrained prejudice against sales people. You've got to work extra hard to overcome that image and prove your good will to clients and prospects.

The Sci-Fi Skinny: *Have You Heard The One...?* by Spider Robinson. American-born Canadian author, b. 1948. This is one of the stories that makes up the Callahan Chronicles, tales of the odd happenings and the odder habitués of Callahan's Crosstime Saloon, including aliens, time-travelers, vampires, empaths, talking dogs and a musician that one suspects might be Robinson's alter-ego. Robinson is a punster of the highest degree, and the pun that serves as the through-line in this story is one of, if not the best, ever put to paper. (If you just can't get it, shoot me an e-mail and I'll explain.) Robinson is also the latter-day answer to Robert Heinlein- see his *Rah, Rah, R.A.H.* essay from 1980 that has appeared in a number of collections, such as *Time Travelers Strictly Cash*, and his handling of *Variable Star*, a novel left behind by Heinlein himself. Robinson was tapped for the project, and allowed to make it his own as much as it is Heinlein's. He did a good job on it, and it's something that they both could/can be proud of.

Lesson 5

The Sci-Fi: *War of the Worlds.* **Radio play adaptation by Orson Welles, of the novel by H.G. Wells**

The Sci-Fi Sitch: When Orson Welles was approached with the idea of doing *War of the Worlds* on the Mercury Theater on the Air radio show, it didn't excite him. So he spiced it up a bit, and made it so the first section emulated radio newscasts of the day: dance music interrupted by simulated bulletins and on-the-scene reports of a Martian invasion of New Jersey. It was perfectly valid and innovative entertainment. But anyone who wasn't tuned in to the beginning of the broadcast missed the notice that this was just a radio play, a dramatization, and some listeners legitimately thought the "news reports" were real. Another announcement about the true nature of the broadcast didn't take place until nearly an hour into the show, so there was a big window of opportunity for listeners to miss the disclaimer and take the fiction as reality.

The Sales Sitch: Some people just don't have an ounce of skepticism in them. Or at least it seems that way when it comes to their believing all the outlandish claims of your competition. (When it's your turn at bat, these same people might very well argue with you if you were to state something as factual as the *color* of your product, let alone its benefits, but that's a different lesson.) These people are more than happy to accept and internalize anything that your competitor has to say about his or her product or service, and it's your job to get them to slow down, take a deep breath, and perform a bit of critical analysis on what is being said.

"Competitor X guarantees weekly service visits," says the client. Impressive, if true. But competitor X lives two hours away, and there is a mountain pass between here and there that is routinely closed during the winter months. I, however, live thirty minutes away across town. Let's think for a moment; how likely is it that Competitor X can REALLY provide more regular service visits than I can?

Or, "Competitor X just told me that their company is acquiring your company." Yes, I had heard that rumor, too, and I spoke with my manager about it last week. There's been some talk of a merger, but the time-frame has no impact on this project. Not to put down Competitor X, but either she's not quite up on the latest developments, or else she's trying to rush you into something without your having all the data.

A New York Tribune columnist's comments on the Welles War of the Worlds broadcast also apply to sales. "A few effective voices, accompanied by sound effects, can convince … people of a totally unreasonable, completely fantastic proposition…"

The Sales and Sci-Fi Lesson: Customers and prospects are susceptible to believing even the most unrealistic claims of your competition, if they are presented with enough flash and sparkle. Encourage clients and prospects to examine all proposals and claims (both yours *and* your competitors') with a clear head and critical eye.

The Sci-Fi Skinny: Orson Welles, American writer, director, actor, producer, 1915-1985 *and* H.G. Wells, English author, 1866-1946.

Welles adapted Wells's (ha, see what I did there?) story of an invasion from Mars into a radio play for Mercury Theater, with simulated live newscasts of the attack. It wasn't the first time such a simulation had been performed, but a number of factors- the timing of the disclaimers, the format of other broadcasts, the sound effects- led a number of people to believe that the invasion was real, and to panic. Following the event, newspapers carried reports of mass hysteria, even claiming that deaths had resulted from the panicked reactions of the listeners, but it seems that these accounts themselves were probably overblown. None of the lawsuits for mental anguish or personal injury were found to have merit. Immediately after, Orson Welles was vilified as some sort of manipulative character who sought to deceive the public and cause terror in the streets, but as it turned out, the War of the Worlds episode was one of his steps to worldwide fame.

Lesson 6

The Sci-Fi: *Planet of the Apes.* **Movie directed by Franklin J. Schaffner, written by Michael Wilson and Rod Serling, from the novel by Pierre Boulle.**

The Sci-Fi Sitch: A group of astronauts crash-lands on a planet and eventually they discover that it's a topsy-turvy world where apes are the civilized and dominant lifeform, while humans are widely regarded as no more than fairly intelligent animals, varmints and pests that raid the crops of the apes. It isn't long before it's down to just Charlton Heston surviving from among the astronauts, and he is captured and held in a cage for a science experiment by one of the chimpanzee scientists. A throat injury has left him unable to speak and thus prove his intelligence, but Heston eventually convinces the kindly chimp scientist and her archaeologist fiancé that he is "smarter than the average human." Once he regains his voice, he talks them into letting him escape the ape city and flee to the archaeology dig that holds the clues to the planet's past, and the secret history of both simian and human cultures.

The Sales Sitch: A salesperson may often feel about their prospects and clients much as Charlton Heston feels about the Planet of the Apes: the world has gone crazy, and the animals are running the zoo. What sales rep hasn't felt like screaming "It's a madhouse! A madhouse!" while getting hosed down by the monkeys that are in control of everything? At times, it feels as if logic makes no difference to these people, no matter how it is presented, no matter what facts you have to back it up. Heston can *prove* that he is intelligent, but the ape authorities refuse to accept it. You can *prove* that your product is the best choice for a prospect, but the powers that be will still choose to purchase the inferior offering from the competitor.

But Heston manages to acquire an ally within the system. As it turns out, his ally doesn't really have much power, and the movie doesn't really end on a very uplifting note, but at least he ends up free and on his own, instead of dissected in a science lab, and it's because he was able to cultivate a friendship with one of the 'people' who were a part of the power structure. In sales, this can be a junior decision-maker, a gatekeeper, or even just a rank-and-file worker. Having a contact on the inside, an ally within the apes, can serve to provide you with a two-way pipeline of information. It can let you know what kinds of decisions are being made in the organization, and it can give you a vehicle to deliver new information to the company… if not *to* the decision-makers, at least *near* them. And best-case scenario, someday that ally may get bumped up into the decision-maker role. (Really! Sometimes dreams do come true!)

The Sales and Sci-Fi Lesson: Cultivate an ally within the target organization. Someone, anyone, who is an insider and is sympathetic to your cause.

The Sci-Fi Skinny: The basis for the movie of Planet of the Apes is the 1963 French novel, "La Planète des singes" by Pierre Boulle. The screenplay was initially written by Twilight Zone's Rod Serling, but his high-tech version was replaced by one with a more primitive ape society, in order to keep costs down. The iconic ending of the film, however, is pure Serling, and he is still officially credited as a writer. *Planet of the Apes,* coming out in the same year as the movie *2001: A Space Odyssey,* helped to mark a turning point in Sci-Fi film, in no small part due to Charlton Heston's presence. Kim Hunter and Roddy McDowall rocked the film, too. The movie was an incredible hit, spawning not just four (four!) sequels in less than three years (1970-1973), but a Saturday morning cartoon show, a television show, comic books, and a pair of movies that have been labeled a 're-make' and a 're-boot'in the new millenium. Plus, the ape makeup was so cutting-edge, it garnered a special Academy Award.

Lesson 7

The Sci-FI: *"If This Goes On---"* **Novel by Robert Heinlein.**

The Sci-FI Sitch: Near the end of the Crazy Years in Heinlein's Future History, America is no longer the land of the free, but instead has become a theocratic dictatorship. John Lyle is a young graduate of West Point military academy, a guardsman in the Angels of the Lord, the personal guards of the current Prophet Incarnate. Lyle gradually comes to learn that the Theocracy is corrupt and hypocritical, and switches his allegiance to an underground rebel group, the Cabal.

At one point, Lyle has to take on the identity of another member of the Cabal; he has to travel across the country, and the Theocracy's police state is actively on the lookout for traitor John Lyle. So with the help of plastic surgery and acting lessons, he assumes the identity of Adam Reeves, commercial traveler in textiles— a textiles salesman, or in the vernacular of the day, a textiles drummer.

The Sales Sitch: John Lyle says of his experience in sales; "…I discovered that there was more to it than carrying around samples and letting a retailer make his choice… Before I finished I acquired a new respect for business men. I had always thought that buying and selling was simple; I was wrong again." And he doesn't just have to take on the Reeves identity; he has to cover the sales route as well, in order for the under-cover ruse to work. "I found that I got as much pleasure out of persuading some hard-boiled retailer that he should increase his line of yard goods as I ever had from military work… Selling isn't just a way to eat; it's a game, it's fun." John Lyle even manages to beat Reeves' sales quota. And I think I know why. Have you ever been in a situation where your manager goes on a sales call with you to a particularly stubborn prospect or client, and manages to wrangle a sweet sales deal, when you've been working the project forever without making any headway? It isn't necessarily that your manager is all that much of a better salesperson than you are— but you are hungry and desperate for this deal, while to your manager, it's just another deal that one of his or her reps is having trouble with. It's not the manager's neck on the line, it's yours. And so the manager can approach the prospect or client with a more detached attitude, without the smell of desperation. Win or lose, the manager doesn't really ever have to deal with the person ever again, so there's no reason to take it too seriously. The manager can even try some really radical sales pitch, because if it blows up, oh well, back to the drawing board. John Lyle is in the same situation in this story. Sales isn't really his life, it's just an act. So he has less emotional investment in the sale, and ironically, this attitude can lead to more and better sales.

The Sales and Sci-Fi Lesson: "Selling isn't just a way to eat; it's a game, it's fun." And if it isn't, then things are getting too serious-- you need to take a step back from it all and reduce the pressure a little bit.

The Sci-Fi Skinny: *"If This Goes On – "* by Robert A. Heinlein. American author, 1907-1988. This story was first published in shorter form as a two-part serial in 1940 in the magazine *Astounding Science-Fiction* under the name *" – Vine and Fig Tree – "*. The expanded/slightly revised novel was included in the collection *Revolt in 2100* in 1953 and in 1967's collection *The Past Through Tomorrow*. According to Bill Patterson, in his extremely thorough article about the story, the original novella ended with John Lyle leaving the military after the successful revolution, and becoming a textiles salesman(!)

This story also contains one of Heinlein's best and most influential quotes. Patterson calls it the first of the "quotable Heinlein," and Damon Knight, in his introduction to *The Past Through Tomorrow*, cites this quote from among the entire (to that time) Future History collection. "When any government, or any church for that matter, undertakes to say to its subjects, 'This you may not read, this you must not see, this you are forbidden to know,' the end result is tyranny and oppression, no matter how holy the motives. Mighty little force is needed to control a man whose mind has been hoodwinked; contrariwise, no amount of force can control a free man, a man whose mind is free. No, not the rack, not fission bombs, not anything – you can't conquer a free man; the most you can do is kill him."

Lesson 8

The Sci-Fi: *The Invisible Man.* **Novel by H.G. Wells.**

The Sci-Fi Sitch: An English university science student discovers a way to turn himself invisible. But while he has envisioned a life of mystery and power by virtue of being able to move about unseen, it turns out to be a difficult and ultimately fatal condition. He is exposed to the elements when invisible (and thus, unclothed). He arouses suspicion when bundled up enough, including hands and face, to interact with people. In the end, all turn against the Invisible Man, and he is killed while trying to escape from his pursuers.

The Sales Sitch: H.G. Wells was more making a comment on what a person might do were there no consequences to their actions, no punishment for breaking the rules, than he was speaking to the reality of sales. And he kind of stacked the deck for the story, too; Griffin, the Invisible Man, was a stinker even before he became invisible. In order to fund his research, he stole his father's money and contributed directly to the father's suicide. And he wanted to become invisible for the power it would gain him. This wasn't some kindly old scientist who turned bad after being tempted by the ability of invisibility; this was a bad man who sought after power and came to a bad end. But just as Griffin came to a bad end from being invisible, so will you, as a sales person, come to a similar end by being invisible. If you are invisible, your prospects can't find you and your clients will forget about you. You want to have high profile, you want to be the Visible Man or Visible Woman. When your competitors try to poach your clients, you will still be top-of-mind for your clients, they will know that you care about them, and it will help to rebuff your competition. And if you stay visible to those who are not yet your clients, when your prospects are dissatisfied with their current providers, then they will know that you are there to provide an alternative solution.

The Sales and Sci-Fi Lesson: The sales lesson here is quick and easy. It is *bad* to be *invisible*; out of sight *really is* out of mind.

The Sci-Fi Skinny: *The Invisible Man* by H.G. Wells, English writer, 1866 – 1946. The story initially appeared as a serial, and then was published as a novel in the same year. Mark Rowlands in his *Philosopher at the End of the Universe* notes that the exploration of the concept of morality and invisibility can be traced back to *The Ring of Gyges* in Plato's *Republic*. As previously noted, Griffin was already a not-so-nice guy before becoming invisible, so it's not surprising that once invisible, he might think that the best use for his power was to be able to murder people, and that he might think that a Reign of Terror was a good idea. It would have been interesting to see what would have happened had Wells' title character been a good-ish person before becoming the Invisible Man. Just as with so many other science fiction themes, H.G. Wells set the bar for the 'invisible person' story, and there have been a lot of sci-fi tales, print and screen, that follow his lead, both with re-tellings of the Wells' story and with new explorations of the theme of invisibility.

Lesson 9

The Sci-Fi: *Star Wars, Episodes IV (A New Hope), V (The Empire Strikes Back), and VI (Return of the Jedi).* **Movies created by George Lucas.**

The Sci-Fi Sitch: Long, long ago in a galaxy far, far away, the interstellar government of the Republic has been overthrown by the political machinations of the new Empire. On a backwater planet, a young man named Luke Skywalker dreams of leaving the farm for a life of glory. Upon learning that his true father was a warrior for the old Republic- a Jedi knight- Luke is determined to follow in his footsteps and train as a Jedi. He convinces another former Jedi, a friend of his father's named Obi-Wan "Ben" Kenobi, to introduce him to the ways of the discipline, and after Obi-Wan's death, he travels to a swamp planet to find the Jedi master Yoda in order to complete his Jedi training.

The Sales Sitch: Luke was a rash and brash young man, but when he realized what he wanted, he found mentors and began to learn. It took a long time — three movies in the original Star Wars trilogy — but he kept learning, and kept growing his knowledge and power. When his first mentor couldn't provide any more guidance (Ben Kenobi was, of course killed- I mean, "went to join the Force," mid-way through the first movie), Luke sought out a new teacher in order to continue his studies.

In sales, having a mentor is like having a guide in the wilderness. The mentor can't do your work for you, but can help you determine more effective ways to do your work. When you make mistakes, the mentor can help you to learn from those mistakes, and to help put the situation in perspective. The mentor can suggest new or different directions for you to explore in specific sales campaigns or in your sales career in general.

The Sales and Sci-Fi Lesson: A mentor can be a powerful resource: Study under someone who is already successful and take advantage of their experience and knowledge to help guide you to your goals.

The Sci-Fi Skinny: As author/philosopher Mark Rowlands says about Star Wars in his book *The Philosopher at the End of the Universe*: "A long time ago in a galaxy far, far away … … blah, blah, blah …. What the hell, everyone knows this one anyway." George Lucas, fresh off the success of his film *American Graffiti*, wrote a good vs. evil space opera that created and utilized a brave new world of motion picture special effects. Star Wars went on to be the most influential science fiction event the world has ever seen, and continues to impact audiences beyond the eventual original movie, original trilogy and prequel trilogy, by way of cartoons (that Lucas maintains to be Star Wars canon), novels, and games. With the much vaunted purchase of the Star Wars franchise by Disney, it is estimated that approximately 98.6 percent of the entire universe is now owned by one single entity. To quote Sergeant Calhoun in the movie *Wreck-It Ralph*, "Doomsday and Armageddon just had a baby, and it… is… ugly." Who knows? Maybe this alliance of the two most powerful forces in the galaxy is a good thing. But the Calhoun quote, being from a Starship Trooper-derivative character in a Disney movie, just felt too ironically appropriate to pass up.

Lesson 10

The Sci-Fi: *2001: A Space Odyssey.* **Movie, directed by Stanley Kubrick, written by Stanley Kubrick and Arthur C. Clarke**

The Sci-Fi Sitch: Earth has sent a mission to Jupiter, an expedition to investigate a mysterious black monolith, with a crew of three astronauts in hibernation, two astronauts that stay awake on the years-long journey away from our planet toward the outer reaches of the solar system, and an (essentially) Artificial Intelligence computer named HAL to run the ship. Long story short (looong story), HAL the computer goes crazy and kills off the crew, until the last surviving astronaut manages to get into its brain and shut down HAL's higher computing functions.

The Sales Sitch: Unless your particular type of sales is walking from town to town, selling odds and ends that you have picked up off the side of the road, your job is going to involve computers at some point. For example, in my particular current line, I use a computer program to keep track of the many different variables that go into the final product for my client. Plus, a web application set up by the parent company directs interested prospects to my cell phone number. Plus, my commission is derived by a complex and arcane formula number-crunched by the corporate HALs. In other words, I sell a product and service that has been around since before computers existed, yet every aspect of the job is now computerized, to some degree. In *2001*, HAL very smugly asserted that his line of computers never made a mistake, and if one did exist, it was due to human error. But whether human error or computer error, the information that comes to me from computers very often is wrong. I have to double-check the math when I give a price quote to my clients. I have to keep an eye on the web to be sure that the corporate site has me properly identified to my prospects. I have to *triple*-check that I'm getting all the commission money that I am entitled to. Whether the humans who program them are incompetent or the computers themselves have gone insane, you just can't take the results from your HAL as gospel. I'm not saying you've got to calculate everything on an abacus or anything so extreme as that. I'm just saying that you've got to be aware there can be errors in the info that you get from the electronic brains, and you need to at least check that their results seem to be in the ballpark of the right answers.

The Sales and Sci-Fi Lesson: Be aware that computers can make mistakes. (Or to be more precise, information that you get from computers can be wrong: whether from 'Garbage In, Garbage Out' or from a psychotic computer, wrong is wrong.) Keep an eye on results to be sure they seem to be at least *close* to the amounts or info that you would expect, and be prepared to double- or triple-check the figures if you need to.

The Sci-Fi Skinny: *2001: A Space Odyssey.* 1968 movie written by Stanley Kubrick (American film director, screenwriter, producer, etc., much of his work was done in the United Kingdom, 1928 – 1999) and Arthur C. Clarke (British science fiction writer, 1917 – 2008), directed by Kubrick. Released in 1968, *2001* eventually earned the top spot for highest grossing film of the year. It is based on Clarke's short story *The Sentinel*, and Clarke wrote his novel version of *2001* concurrently with his and Kubrick's work on the movie. The film has become revered as a classic, and a 'serious' work within the genre. While I honor Clarke as a member of the 'Big Three,' joining Heinlein and Asimov, I just can't put this movie on my list of faves. It beats you over the head with the pre-history. Beats you over the head with the secrecy surrounding the discovery of the monolith on the moon. Beats you over the head with the Jupiter voyage, especially the repair scene and the recovery of the dead astronaut scene. Beats you over the head with the interminable psychedelic scenery when Dave the astronaut reaches the Jupiter monolith. This movie is so in love with its own great effects of weightlessness, space travel, etc., that it takes an entire film to present what should have fit into the first twenty minutes, and ends the story at exactly the point where it should really be getting into the meat of it. IMHO. But it's hard to argue against the fact that it did help to bring the genre of science fiction into the mainstream consciousness.

Lesson 11

The Sci-Fi: *The Man Who Sold the Moon.* **Short story by Robert Heinlein.**

The Sci-Fi Sitch: In Heinlein's Future History, D.D. Harriman is a man who desperately wants humanity to travel to the Moon; as a stepping stone to the stars, yes, but also as an affirmation of our progress, our movement forward, our desires and aspirations. And he wants it done his way, in order to keep the moon, and by extension, space travel, from becoming a sticking point in international relations. "Damnation, nationalism should stop at the stratosphere," he states. At first, no one is much interested, because "what's in it for us?" But Harriman is a clever ol' rascal, the veteran of several rough-and-tumble business ventures, and he *really* wants to get to the Moon. He does a lot of things to build quite a buzz about his project, from convincing the 'Moka Coke' company that their rival (a soda company named '6+') has approached him about putting their logo across the face of the moon, to planting stories in the media that uranium and diamonds are common and plentiful on the moon, ours for the taking if we'll only go there and take them. In the end, we have Delos D. Harriman to thank for providing the vision and drive that takes us to Luna, the other planets in our solar system, and beyond.

The Sales Sitch: Harriman was a visionary; he saw the value, and not just in monetary terms, of space travel. But he seemed to be the only one. No one else, not the governments, not the corporations, not the businessmen of the time, could see what he saw. Pitching the Moon to humanity was an uphill battle. So D.D. Harriman changed the playing field. He twisted and mangled the facts and opinions until people came around to his way of thinking. And when they did come around, he made sure that he was the one who could provide the answers and solutions, the pathway to what they now perceived as their new goal. When setting up the dummy corporations and legal precedents that will allow him to lead/guide the world where he wants it to go, Harriman says, "I want the deck stacked so that we win no matter how the cards are dealt."

As a sales manager once similarly put it: "We want to make the playing field level, *but in our favor.*" The situation he had in mind was when the corporate brass of a prospective client company wanted to put the project out for bids. By virtue of a friendship with the manager who would be in charge of the project, it was possible to write the bid specs so that they were equal to all prospective vendors, but just happened to require or request attributes or features in which our company was particularly strong. We influenced the situation so that what the client really wanted was what we had to offer. If a competitor could do a better job of offering what *we* had to offer, they would win the bid; so in that manner, the playing field was level. But the specs were developed with our product in mind, so the playing field was level, in our favor.

The Sales and Sci-Fi Lesson: If you can have influence on what the client thinks they want or need, you should make the playing field level in your favor.

The Sci-Fi Skinny: Robert Anson Heinlein (American writer 1907 – 1988) wrote *The Man Who Sold the Moon* as a classic 'Moses' story; the protagonist guided humanity to the promised land, yet was prohibited from crossing over the river Jordan to partake of its rewards. And I'm not making this up or inferring it; Heinlein specifically uses this language in the story. The 1983 paperback version of *The Past Through Tomorrow* features a cover with Harriman sitting in a nighttime airfield, gazing wistfully at the sky, and he looks strikingly like R.A.H. It's a great cover, one of my favorites. The actual story first appeared, as best as I can tell, as the title story in a 1950 collection of Heinlein shorts, and interestingly enough, is actually a prequel to *Requiem*, this latter story having been published in 1940.

Lesson 12

The Sci-Fi: *Star Trek.* **Movie, directed by J.J. Abrams, written by Roberto Orci and Alex Kurtzman.**

The Sci-Fi Sitch: We all know and love *Star Trek* (the television series in the '60s), *Star Trek* (the motion picture in the '70s), and *Star Trek* (the other movies and syndicated t.v. shows that followed). Or at least we all know them, sometimes the love is not so easy to come by as the recognition is.

But eventually, as we went boldly into the interior of the 21st century, it seemed that the creativity well started to run dry. Popular opinion, at one point, was that without a major reboot, the franchise was dead. Enter J.J. Abrams of *Fringe* and *Lost* to direct the 2009 major revamp (written, not coincidentally, by Abrams' frequent cohorts Orci and Kurtzman). I went in ready to hate it. I'm enough of a fan that I sometimes go to Trek conventions. I don't wear Vulcan ears or recite poety in Klingon or anything, but I'm pretty serious about the canon. So I anticipated not being impressed. I was wrong. They wrote a time-loop into this movie that allows them to do new and fresh stuff with Trek, without ignoring or ripping down the previously established storyline. Not everyone agrees with me, but I think it works. More than that, I think it works brilliantly. (Plus, it's said that some of the plotline originated with the creator himself, Gene Roddenberry, so how can you kick against that?)

In the mid-future, humanity has discovered a warp drive that allows interstellar travel, and Starfleet is Earth's navy in space. As most everyone knows, 'these are the voyages of the starship Enterprise' into 'the final frontier', 'to boldly go' where no one has gone before. But in this 11th film in the franchise, there has been a glitch in time, and a Romulan mining ship gets bumped back into the year 2233, destroys the U.S.S. Kelvin space ship, along with Captain James T. Kirk's father. His wife gives birth to our Captain Kirk on an escape shuttle fleeing from the Romulans. The resulting time/space continuum is one very similar to the one that we are familiar with from the original television series, in that many of the characters that we know live their lives in ways that mesh with the original. But there are differences, just as there would have to be, given that a murderous huge Romulan ship is now out to destroy whatever Federation ships it can find, as well as the planet Vulcan.

The Sales Sitch: At some point in your career, you may need to reboot, revamp, or renovate. You may not want to, and you may think the result will be something you'll hate. But sometimes there is no way to move forward without going back to the beginning and rebuilding your story. It's not something to be undertaken lightly, because you can't do it halfway and then stop. So if you think that you might need to reboot, you also need to take the time to really analyze the why, what, and how of the project. Because once you go with it, you have to go with it all the way. But with brilliance and originality, you could change your career from dead-end and lackluster to new and better than ever.

The sales lesson here is also the story. Or the story is the sales lesson. I'm a guy who believes in canon. You know, the annoying nerd who picks apart any little flaw in continuity from one book or movie to another. Yes, I'm *that guy*. Usually. So I didn't have high hopes for this re-imagining of one of modern science fiction's sacred cows. But Abrams, Orci and Kurtzman boldly went. And boldly made it work.

The Sales and Sci-Fi Lesson: You might need a career revamp in order to continue to have a career. And if you're going to do it, do it right, with time, resources, brilliance and originality. In other words, *boldly go*.

The Sci-Fi Skinny: While Star Wars is arguably the largest science fiction event in history, Star Trek broke ground for science fiction on the screen, and an in-depth discussion of its impact is beyond the scope of the Sci-Fi Skinny. Suffice it to note that the 2009 renovation of the franchise keeps it successfully and profitably trekking on for at least another generation.

Lesson 13

The Sci-Fi: *Star Trek.* **Novelization by Alan Dean Foster of the movie directed by J.J. Abrams.**

The Sci-Fi Sitch: At the Starfleet Academy, there is an infamous training simulation that the cadets must face; the Kobyashi Maru. It is the name of a space freighter that has put out a distress call to which, in the simulation, the cadets must respond. No one can seem to find a way to succeed in the battle situation with which they are presented. Until one James T. Kirk goes through the training exercise and surprisingly, miraculously, unbelievably, beats it. That's the good part; the bad part is that Commander Spock, who programmed the simulation, actually designed it to be unbeatable, in order to present aspiring officers with a no-win situation. Kirk had managed to get a subroutine installed into the program that allowed a *win* situation; he changed the parameters of the exercise. He refused to accept a no-win situation.

The Sales Sitch: Sometimes, there really *is* no way to win the sale. It may be because the client personally just doesn't like you. It may be because your product isn't a good fit. It may be because your product is really and honestly out of the budget range of the prospect. So if there is no way to win in the current situation, then you have to change the parameters. In many cases, this means establishing and maintaining a good, or even great, relationship with the prospect, accepting the fact that you **will not sell to them**, until there is a shift in their needs, their budget, or in your product, to the point where you *can* win the sale. You may need to change the parameters of your situation to more of a long-range timeframe, wherein success is not measured in achieving a sale now, or in this sales cycle, but in the future, several cycles or years down the line. If the situation that is no-win involves a prospect who just *will not* deal with you, even though you may offer the best product and service at the best price, then you may have to change the parameters of the timeframe, and hope to outlast this particular person. But other parameters that you might look at are the obstinate prospect's superiors (Can you pitch to an uber-decision maker? Do the prospect's higher-ups know that the prospect is refusing to go with a superior product just because of personal bias?) or the prospect's client base (Do the prospect's clients, membership, or recipients know that they are paying a higher cost and/or receiving an inferior product just because of the whim of that decision maker?)

The Sales and Sci-Fi Lesson: Don't accept a no-win situation. When faced with one, change the parameters. It may take a lot of creativity, or an entirely different perspective, but it can be done.

The Sci-Fi Skinny: In the original Star Trek, we knew Captain Kirk as the charismatic commander of the starship Enterprise, at a point well into his Starfleet career, and the fact that he was the only cadet to ever beat the Kobyashi Maru simulation was a tale from his earlier days, mentioned only in passing, with the implication that he did so because of a superior or inspired grasp of tactics and strategy. In the Abrams reboot and subsequent Foster novelization, we see the young Cadet Kirk and the young Commander Spock at the academy, and learn that the storyline involves Kirk beating the system through what some might call subterfuge, others might call cheating, but that I choose to interpret as changing the parameters of the situation. And it is an important plot point, because it leads into the animosity between Kirk and Spock that drives a lot of the later action in the story. The in-depth and entertaining way in which Alan Dean Foster (American writer, b. 1946) presents this situation is just what one would expect of ADF, master of the Sci-Fi novelization in general and master of Star Trek novelization in particular.

Lesson 14

The Sci-Fi: Robert Heinlein's first sale. Industry anecdote.

The Sci-Fi Sitch: Robert Heinlein was retired from the military in 1934 as being medically unfit for service, following a bout with pulmonary tuberculosis. In 1938, he ran and lost a campaign as a candidate for California's 59th assembly district. He was in a situation in which many of us have found ourselves: mounting bills, no money, and nothing very promising on our horizon. As the story goes, in October of 1938, a speculative fiction pulp magazine called *Thrilling Wonder Stories* ran a contest for new and unpublished writers. According to his wife, Virginia, RAH "bought some paper for his typewriter and wrote *Life-Line*." It is said that he completed it in four days. But then, instead of submitting the story to *Thrilling Wonder Stories*, he sent it off to *Astounding Science-Fiction*, where genre legend John Campbell accepted and published it.

The Sales Sitch: I have heard two different accounts of why Heinlein sent *Life-Line* to *Astounding* instead of to *Thrilling Wonder*. One is that he recognized that the quality of his story was far above the usual stuff that appeared in *Thrilling Wonder Stories*, and so sent it to a magazine that was more suited to it. The other is that, realizing that *Thrilling Wonder Stories* would be receiving a glut of submissions in response to the contest offer, shrewd ol' Robert A. Heinlein decided to send his story to a different prospect, one that would presumably not be getting as many submissions at this time. Either way, the lesson for a sales professional is that sometimes the best place to prospect for customers isn't the most obvious place. Just because everybody else is pitching to a potential client doesn't mean that that client is really where you should be pitching... either because your product is better suited to a different customer, or because your presentation will make more of an impact with a customer who isn't being inundated by your competition.

The Sales and Sci-Fi Lesson: The most obvious prospect isn't always the *best* prospect.

The Sci-Fi Skinny: This anecdote about Heinlein shows up a lot in the annals of Sci-Fi lore, for a number of reasons. For one, it's just such a great concept; this brilliant fellow, at a time of financial and emotional hardship in his life, sits down and whips out a great story, a story that marks the beginning of one of the most successful science fiction writing careers of the century. For another, it is the exception that proves the rule, the rule being that aspiring writers must toil away at their art and craft for years, even decades, honing their writing and collecting rejection slips before breaking into the business.

Lesson 15

The Sci-Fi: *A Plague of Demons.* **Novel by Keith Laumer.**

The Sci-Fi Sitch: Super-secret-agent John Bravais discovers that an alien race has infiltrated the U.N. and the governments of the Earth in a mid-future (this book was published in 1965). They seem to be killing people and stealing their brains, maneuvering nations into armed conflicts in order to create situations in which they can make their creepy harvests. In the course of his discovery and his work against these aliens, Bravais receives both mental conditioning and a physical overhaul, à la the Six-Million-Dollar Man. He is almost a superman; he is definitely super cool. He rocks, but... the aliens still finally kill him. Oh, the story doesn't end there, because they steal his brain, and put it into an alien war tank, and he ends up fighting against them on some alien planet. But as a futuristic giant tank, not in his rocking supercool souped-up human body that he had for much of the book.

The Sales Sitch: John Bravais had a top-of-the-line product. He was a one-man army, a killing machine in a war against the aliens. He knew more about them than they knew about him. In a one-on-one confrontation, he had the advantage. And yet they still killed him off. They ganged up on him and ripped him apart. In the same way that your top-of-the-line product can still get picked off by the brain-stealing scavengers that beset you every day out there in the sales world. Powerful, unfortunately, is not invincible.

The Sales and Sci-Fi Lesson: While it is much better to represent the best product in the field than it is to represent an inferior product, the fact of being the *best* does not make you *bullet-proof.* Watch out for the scavengers who will do their best to take you down, no matter how.

The Sci-Fi Skinny: *A Plague of Demons* (Keith Laumer, American writer, 1925 – 1993) was published as a novel in 1965, and a shorter version appeared serially in *IF magazine* in 1964. The 1970s Warner Books editions featured on the cover a picture of a red alien war tank with the Earth in the sky behind it and a human skull in the foreground, with the top sheared off and writhing, tentacle-y, mass, sitting right where the brain should be... Coolest. Cover. Ever.

Lesson 16

The Sci-Fi: *Valor's Choice.* **Novel by Tanya Huff.**

The Sci-fi Sitch: Staff Sgt. Torin Kerr's combat-hardened platoon and their new, green second looey have been sent to babysit a diplomatic mission, the delegates of which are trying to convince a new and unaligned alien race (human-sized martial lizards) to join the good guys of the universe-- the Confederation-- instead of the baddies-- the Others. The differences between the enlisted Marines, the officers, and the diplomats notwithstanding, Staff closes ranks throughout the story in defense of the Marines, of the Confederation, and of humans. This philosophy of sticking together, of group loyalty (even when faced with evidence that her superiors set Staff and her troops up to be ambushed and slaughtered), ultimately saves the day, the diplomatic mission, and by implication, the future of the Confederation.

The Sales Sitch: Like the staff sergeant, even when you feel that the company is treating you badly, you can't badmouth it in public. Even if there is a devastating situation that is your manager's fault, or even comes from higher up the food chain, make sure not to complain to clients, prospects, or anyone else outside your organization. If you air your grievances about the higher-ups in public, it makes it look as if you are trying to shift blame and weasel out of responsibility. And if, the prospect wonders, the rep will shift blame off of herself or himself onto the company, might they not also, in certain situations, try to shift blame for a problem onto a client? Why would a client want to work with someone who might, when the chips are down, try to blame the client for a sales rep error? Or even if you have a great relationship with the prospect or client, and they know/believe you that the responsibility for the problems lies with the corporate brass, and not with you, well then, why would they really want to do business with an organization that has such incompetence in its chain of command?

The Sales and Sci-Fi Lesson: Don't badmouth the company- you have more to *lose* than to *gain* by blaming management or other people in your organization for problems or errors.

The Sci-Fi Skinny: Tanya Huff (Canadian writer, b. 1957) is known for her several fantasy series more than she is for her one Sci-Fi series, but her military science-fiction series, the Valor Confederation, rings pretty true to my ear (I do have some military experience. Not tons, but some). *Valor's Choice* was published in 2000, and was included in an omnibus collection in 2006, *A Confederation of Valor,* which included the first two novels of the series, *Valor's Choice* and *The Better Part of Valor,* the latter of which was published in 2002.

Lesson 17

The Sci-Fi: *Inception.* **Movie, written and directed by Christopher Nolan**

The Sci-Fi Sitch: This is a story about being able to travel into, and to some degree, control the dreams of oneself and of others. The lead character is an acknowledged expert and innovator in the field, a young master of the theory and implementation of the process. In the movie, he brings a new member onto his team, a young woman, and he begins to train her in dream control and dream architecture. One of the important bits of advice that he gives her is to select a small token or tchotchke- his is a small metal spinning top, almost like a dreidel- that she can use to focus her mind, anchor her reality, and help her to delineate the dream world from the real world.

The Sales Sitch: Thoughts, ideas, and feelings can all be inspirational and help you to focus on and to achieve your sales goals. But they are intangible. Sometimes a physical representation of your self-confidence and goals is beneficial. Mine happens to be a heavy gold ring that was presented to me upon my induction into my company's sales recognition club, a honor given when a sales rep reaches a certain amount of revenue. When I have setbacks or discouragements in my sales life, I can twist this ring on my finger, or even take it off and close my fist around it, taking comfort in its weight and solidity. It reminds me of my past successes and is an affirmation that despite any problems I might be experiencing right now, I am a good, even great, sales rep; it focuses my mind and helps me to delineate my current slump from the reality of my true sales abilities and accomplishments.

The Sales and Sci-Fi Lesson: Select a small, physical representation, a token that you can use to anchor your success, to focus your mind on the positives, to help keep you upbeat during tough times.

The Sci-Fi Skinny: Christopher Nolan (British writer (with dual American citizenship), director, b. 1970) is firmly ensconced as one of the most interesting individuals in modern Spec-Fic film, having written and directed *The Prestige* and *Inception* (eight Academy Award nominations, ended up taking four), having successfully rebooted the Batman films, and taking on the same task for Superman. And in addition to *influencing* the Sci-Fi film genre, he's a *product* of the Sci-Fi film genre, citing Stanley Kubrick, *2001*, Ridley Scott, and *Blade Runner* as inspirations, and he works with actors who are making their own impacts on Sci-Fi film, such as Hugh Jackman, Joseph Gordon-Levitt and Christian Bale.

Lesson 18

The Sci-Fi: *Firefly.* **Television series by Josh Whedon.**

The Sales Sitch: The setting is the 2500s, after a civil war in which the planets and forces seeking greater freedom and more independence and rights were brought back under the control of the Alliance. Malcolm "Mal" Reynolds (a former Browncoat, as the rebels are known) is the captain of a Firefly-class spaceship, a cargo ship that he uses to eke out a living in interplanetary transport. He and his crew (including another veteran soldier buddy from the war) take on a lot of smuggling, robbery and other extra-legal work, particularly if it will serve as a way to thumb their noses at the Alliance authorities that be.

Crewmember Jayne Cobb is portrayed as a fairly amoral mercenary, not usually coming across as too bright or sentimental, but very competent at his job (which is often beating people up, or even killing them). He has a special weapon that he likes to use ("It is my very favorite gun.") and it actually shows up in a number of situations in the series. As noted in wikia devoted to the show, "He had named his favorite and most powerful gun, a Callahan full-bore auto lock with customized trigger." (Its name is Vera.) "He acquired it after killing the previous owner, one of six assassins trying to kill him."

The Sales Sitch: Sales is not an arena in which to be understated or subtle. Sometimes sales reps are afraid of coming on too strong to a prospect, but you need to go in with your best offer, to show your full strength in order to show up the competition, or even better, to blow them completely away and to establish your own primacy. You need to bring out the big gun.

If you come into the fray with anything less than your best, there are a number of results that you can expect, and none of them are good. First and foremost, you can lose the sale to your competitor who has made a better offer. Their best, or even their second-best, might be better than the less-than-best offer that you brought to the table. But if you go in with your best, then even if you lose the account, you know that it wasn't because you mis-judged how much effort to put into it… you'll know that the deal was beyond your control no matter what, that you didn't lose it because of anything you could have done differently.

And if you DO win the account with a less-than-best offer, you might be encouraging your competition to keep sniping at you… they may feel that they only missed beating you out by a little bit, and that they are still in the game when the sales opportunity cycles back around. The client may feel this way, too, whereas if your proposal really crushed the competition, both may feel that your competitor just isn't in your league.

Another bad situation that can arise from winning an account with a second-best offer is that if and when there is a problem with the sales or service, it may give the client a reason to take the business elsewhere the next time around. They may think they don't really have *that* much to lose, since your deal was only a little bit better than the other provider's offer. On the other hand, if your deal was *so* much better than that of your closest competitor, the client may be willing to put up with a few minor setbacks… after all, they did get *such* a great deal on the product.

The Sales and Sci-Fi Lesson: Go in with your big guns, your best deal. Always. Or risk losing to someone else who does.

The Sci-Fi Skinny: *Firefly*, the short-lived but much-loved fan favorite television show from Joss Whedon (American writer, director, producer, b. 1964) is often (very accurately) called a 'Sci-Fi Western.' The civil war in the storyline, while not over slavery, is over states' (or planets') rights, and many of the planets visited by the crew of Serenity are frontier civilizations reminiscent of the early American West. Like Christopher Nolan, Whedon is another individual who has, by virtue of originality and creativity, worked his way up to an impactful position in Sci-Fi film. In addition to screen works (big screen and small screen) including *Buffy, Angel, Dr. Horrible* and *The Avengers*, Whedon has also made a name for himself in the comic book field. *Firefly* ran 14 episodes in 2002-2003, and led to a movie, *Serenity*, in 2005.

Lesson 19

The Sci-Fi: *The Matrix.* **Movie by the Wachowskis.**

The Sci-Fi Sitch: In *The Matrix*, most of humanity exists as rows of comatose individuals, encased in pods and used as batteries, a power source, for the Artificial Intelligence computer that has taken over the world. These people think they are living their lives in the 1980s, going about their business and being regular people, but everything they are experiencing is just a part of the Matrix program. Some people have broken free from the illusion, and live a rebellious, refugee existence, trying to bring down the computer, the Matrix, and live real lives, rather than simulated experiences while their bodies provide power to the system. Keanu Reeves plays the role of Neo, someone who may or may not be a prophecied savior of humanity. In the movie, one of the crew members of the rebel ship that has retrieved Neo from the Matrix ends up betraying the rebellion and his fellow free humans. He strikes a deal with the computer, because he would rather live a false life inside his own head, one where he can eat steak and enjoy luxury, than live a real life that involves the hardships and sacrifices of fighting the system.

The Sales Sitch: Your prospects may also prefer the status quo, the ease of going along with the way things are, rather than the effort that it would take to switch to your product or service. Even more than that, if they introduce a change into the system (that is, whatever you're offering them), and it goes bad, they can be blamed for it, whereas if they just stay with the way things are, even if it's not so great, no blame will be attached to them. So you really need to make it a clear-cut choice of **What's In It For Me** to the client; you need to make it very plain that the rewards of change far outweigh the rewards of remaining with the current situation. While features are always good, you need to show how these features equal benefits, the bigger benefits the better, for the client.

The Sales and Sci-Fi Lesson: Prospects don't move out of their status quo comfort zone for nothing. You need to give them a very good reason to undertake the effort of change.

The Sci-Fi Skinny: The Watchowskis are the siblings (and directors, screenwriters, producers) Lana (formerly Larry) (b. 1965) and Andy (b. 1967) Watchowski. *The Matrix* in 1999 was their second film, for which they were awarded the Saturn Award for Best Director. Their other films in Spec-Fic include *V for Vendetta*, *Speedracer* and *Cloud Atlas*. In addition to spawning two sequels and a number of books, games, etc., the Matrix film is notable for developing a photography technique known as bullet-time, a slow-motion swing-around in real time. The Matrix trilogy is also a significant entry in the Sci-Fi film career of Keanu Reeves, which also includes *Johnny Mnemonic, A Scanner Darkly,* and *The Day the Earth Stood Still.*

20: The Sci-Fi: The Cover Art of Sweet, Whelan, Vallejo, etc. Industry anecdote.

The Sci-Fi Sitch: Growing up in small, rural town in the West, I quickly worked my way through the limited science-fiction section of the local library. So when we would make a visit into the big city, once every couple of months or so, I would bring along the spending money I had earned from chores and splurge on a new book. (Well, maybe not a *big* city, but at least a city. Put it this way, it did have a couple of bookstores in it, which was a couple more than the little town out in our neck of the sticks.) But deciding just what book to buy could be a daunting task, given the wide selection from which to choose. One way that I could pick a new book was, of course, to buy something by one of my go-to writers, like Robert Heinlein, Isaac Asimov, or Edgar Rice Burroughs. But what about when I wanted to branch out?

What I did then was to look at the cover art on the books and authors that I knew and liked, and then searched for new authors whose covers had the same type of art. In this manner, Boris Vallejo led me from Tarzan's jungles to Zelazny's Amber. Michael Whelan guided me from the red planet Barsoom to the dragon-filled skies of Pern. Darrell K. Sweet took me from Heinlein's *Tunnel in the Sky*, *Time for the Stars*, and more, to batches of other Del Rey books by other writers. In other words, yes, I made a habit of judging books by their covers.

The Sales Sitch: And I'm not the only one. When someone is being asked to invest money (their own, or their company's) into a new product or service, they really do want some indication that they are going to get something of quality in return. And the appearance, the packaging, (the cover), is the most visible and immediate representation of that quality. When a prospect or a new client sees an outward appearance that is obviously the result of care and attention, something that both you and they can be proud of, they think to themselves, "Well, so far, so good!" before even getting to the essence of the product. But if their first sight of the product is a shabby, poorly-executed or amateurish "cover," you have already primed them into a negative expectation. Even if the product itself is flawless, you've already put yourself at a disadvantage. And when I talk about the appearance of the product, that includes *your* appearance as well; you are what you represent, and what you look like will influence what your client thinks about your *product*.

The Sales and Sci-Fi Lesson: First impressions count, because a person who is about to spend money *does and will* judge a book by its cover.

The Sci-Fi Skinny: Boris Vallejo (Peruvian-born American artist, b. 1941) is known for his paintings of larger-than-life brawny warriors, busty barbarians and epic creatures. It's a style very well suited for action fantasy, such as Tarzan or Conan, but his work has also graced the covers of some science-fiction as well, including books by authors such as Philip Jose Farmer, Frederik Pohl, Theodore Sturgeon, and some Star Trek novelizations. Vallejo was nominated for Hugos in 1979 and 1980, and was a guest of honor at the 69th annual World Science Fiction Convention.

Michael Whelan (American artist, b. 1950) started out selling to Marvel Comics, Ace Books, and even Harlan Ellison, and has had a steady and productive career ever since. He was nominated for his first Hugo in 1978, and won his first one in 1980. He has been associated with the Edgar Rice Burroughs John Carter of Mars series, Stephen King's Dark Tower stories, and has done work for covers of books by Asimov, Clarke and Heinlein. He was guest of honor at the World Science Fiction Conventions in 1998 and 2007. He has been inducted into the Science Fiction Hall of Fame and has been awarded the Solstice Award from the Science Fiction Writers of America. And finally, when Darrell K. Sweet passed away in 2011, leaving the 14th and final book in the Wheel of Time series without cover art, publisher TOR asked Whelan to do the art for *A Memory of Light*. According to his bio, he "strove faithfully to capture the hero's likeness and the mood of the series in the Whelan style, while remaining true to Sweet's vision."

Darrell K. Sweet (American artist, 1934 – 2011) was, perhaps, more known for fantasy art, such as his work on the Piers Anthony Xanth series and Robert Jordan's Wheel of Time books, than for his science-fiction art, but he did do several Sci-Fi covers, including art for books by Robert Heinlein, Philip K. Dick, Larry Niven/Jerry Pournelle, Frederik Pohl, Alan Dean Foster, L. Sprague De Camp, James P. Hogan and Isaac Asimov. Sweet was nominated for a Hugo in 1983.

Lesson 21

The Science Fiction: The Self-Promotion of Isaac Asimov. Industry anecdote.

The Sci-Fi Sitch: At a certain period in history, the name Isaac Asimov was synonymous with the phrase Science-Fiction. But Asimov wasn't the only Sci-Fi author around, so why him? Of the Big Three of the Golden Age of Science Fiction, why does a Google search of Robert Heinlein or Arthur C. Clarke come back with between three and four million results for either of these giants of SF, but over *eight million* for their contemporary, the inimitable Dr. A?

Well, part of it is that he produced like a madman. And he subsequently self-promoted like a madman. He wrote SF, he wrote mysteries, he wrote fiction, he wrote non-fiction, he wrote essays, he wrote science, he wrote reviews. He declared himself adequate to the task of explaining the Bible, of explaining Shakespeare, and of explaining science to the world. He had his name on a science-fiction magazine. He was a science professor and a historian. He had published works in all ten of the major categories of the Dewey decimal system. In fact, I have often thought that Isaac Asimov was the twentieth century's version of Benjamin Franklin.

The Sales Sitch: In addition to being smart, smart, smart, Asimov was also smart. He didn't wait around for other people to declare him to be an expert in things. He declared it himself, and then acted to prove it by writing on the subjects, by becoming the acknowledged expert that he had claimed himself to be. Although he hated flying, and so didn't make many of the rounds of events that weren't on the East Coast, he was a great networker at the events that he did attend. So he got his name known both to the loyal fandom of SF, and to the general public at large. He became the go-to guy for the media if they wanted a comment on science or science fiction. And as noted earlier, even today, a Google search turns up more than twice as many results on Asimov than on the other two members of the Triumvirate of the Golden Age. This is a how you want to be as a sales rep. When someone thinks of your product, you want to hold the position of Top of Mind Awareness; that is, when someone thinks of your product, you want them to think of you. If the local media is doing a story that involves your product or service, you want to be the name in the Rolodex that comes up as an expert in the field. When someone turns to Google to find out about your industry, you want to be the person that is highlighted by the search engine.

The Sales and Sci-Fi Lesson: Don't wait for others to become aware of you. While part of being well-known for what you do is to do what you do well, the other part of being well-known is to *make* yourself well-known.

The Sci-Fi Skinny: Isaac Asimov was born in Russia in either 1919 or 1920, but his family moved to America when he was three, and he grew up in Brooklyn. He began writing while still in his teens, and he was one of John W. Campbell's stable of writers; his story *Nightfall* was selected by the SFWA membership as the best science-fiction story of all time. Asimov went on to earn a doctorate in chemistry, to teach at Boston University, and to become one of the most famous and influential of SF's Golden-Agers. His Foundation series and his robotics and their positronic brains show up regularly in references- and in the genre- still today.

Lesson 22

The Sci-Fi: *Off Armageddon Reef.* **Novel by David Weber.**

The Sci-Fi Sitch: In 2378, spacefaring humanity is up against the wall, desperately trying to find a way to survive against the alien Gbaba. The last-ditch strategy is to flee to some far-off planet and eschew the technology that has been the neon "Here we are!" signal to the enemy. The plan works, but there are two factions among the colony leaders, and the winning side installs an anti-tech religious mindset into the brainwiped colonists when they are unthawed from the interstellar exodus. Nearly 900 years later, the last of the losing side awakens to find herself as a sort of an android, hidden away as an ace-in-the-hole by the moderates amongst the colony leaders, who opposed the brainwashing of the rank and file and were eventually killed off. In fact, the names of the moderates in this new society are synonymous with the Devil, while the leaders of the successful faction are remembered as literal Angels. But in this new anti-tech society, the technology that is at the command of the woman whose consciousness inhabits the android body (including the android itself and tools and resources such as satellite monitoring) make her almost superhuman. Using these powers, she sides with a small kingdom that embodies the values of her faction, a kingdom that is about to be conquered by the combined might of the Church and the Church's subordinate secular forces, representing the values of the anti-tech faction. By using her satellite monitors and electronic bugging tools, our protagonist knows all of the opponents' battle plans as soon as they are decided, and is able to guide her kingdom's military forces to exactly the right places to win a crushing victory, to win both the battles *and* the war.

The Sales Sitch: Knowledge (of your opponent's resources and plans) is power. If you have access to the products and services of your competitors, you can analyze them for their weaknesses and exploit them, pointing their shortcomings out to the prospects. You can even analyze their strengths, and downplay or counter them. If you know the competition's plans, you can develop strategies to counteract and defeat them. For example, what their bid or proposal will be, how much incentive they are willing to offer or where they will be prospecting. If you are particularly close with an existing client, they can really help you out by clueing you in on the specifics of the offerings of your competitors whenever your counterparts from another company attempt to poach the client from you.

On the other hand, you also have to be careful not to let your own information fall into your competition's hands. I once knew a sales rep that loved to Tweet about where she was going, who she was meeting, and where she had been. All the competition had to do was to follow her online posts and they knew her entire itinerary. The competition could follow right on her heels with meetings designed to exaggerate her weaknesses and to present a better deal than she had offered. I myself have a Twitter account that is not followed by clients and prospects, but by professionals in the field, including my competition, and I have, on occasion, given misleading info via online posts when I knew that a specific competitor and I were both on the short list for a particular deal.

The Sales and Sci-Fi Lesson: Knowledge is power; use the flow and control of knowledge, both incoming and outgoing, to gain an advantage over your competitors.

The Sci-Fi Skinny: David Weber is the author of the NYT best-selling Honor Harrington series, as well as many, many other books, including some set in Keith Laumer's Bolo universe. Since *Off Armageddon Reef* was published in 2007, Weber has published a new Safehold series novel at a fairly steady rate of one per year. Weber's work is published by both Baen and by Tor.

Lesson 23

The Sci-Fi: *Fahrenheit 451.* **Novel by Ray Bradbury**

The Sci-Fi Sitch: This classic novel of book banning is set in the near future, when books of all sorts have been outlawed, and firemen are not here to help humanity by putting out house fires – all of the homes are fireproof-- but instead, exist to track down and incinerate those tools of the subversives: books. And if the subversives end up charbroiled in the process, well then, they brought that on themselves, now didn't they? The novel takes its name from the temperature at which paper ignites, and the storyline follows one of the firemen, Montag, through his transformation from a good, order-following public servant, to a confused soul, intrigued by the forbidden books, and finally to a fugitive from society, living outside of civilization in the country, along with the other rebels who dare to read and preserve literature. But these refugees don't carry the actual books around with them- each person has memorized a book, and they keep the world's greatest works intact by passing the written word along in an oral tradition.

The Sales Sitch: This novel has become a favorite of the standard-bearers in the fight against censorship and book-banning. But the lesson for the sales rep is not quite so lofty. Instead, it is a reminder of the persistence of the written word, be it on paper or in a digital file. In *Fahrenheit 451*, several noted works of literature survive and thrive, through even a societal purge that seeks to eliminate books. So too will your memos and e-mails survive even your most stringent efforts to delete them. In other words, don't write it down if you don't want it to exist in that form throughout eternity. When you write a bid proposal or make a service guarantee, you had better be prepared to stand by it, because if you don't, it will turn up when you least expect it and bite you in the behind.

The Sales and Sci-Fi Lesson: If you put it in writing (on paper or digitally), you had better plan on it being around forever. If you write it, you will need to own it.

The Sci-Fi Skinny*: Fahrenheit 451*, published in 1953, was perhaps the most well-known work of Ray Bradbury (American writer, 1920 - 2012), along with his *Martian Chronicles* and *The Illustrated Man*. As mentioned, *Fahrenheit 451* is annually trotted out by the anti-censorship movement, almost as a manifesto of the cause. So it's worth noting what the author himself had to say about it. Journalist Amy E. Boyle Johnston interviewed Bradbury shortly after he was awarded the Pulitzer Prize in 2007. She reported that he was fairly emphatic that *F451* was ***not*** a story about government censorship, but instead, an indictment of television's soul-suckingness and its role in the death of literature.

Bradbury is also famous, or perhaps infamous, for refusing to allow ebook or digital versions of his works. Shortly before his death in 2012, though, he made the news again for a publication contract renewal that included an ebook provision. It seems that he was forced into allowing for digital publication as a condition of renewal, but at the same time, made the digital publication contingent upon the publisher, Simon & Schuster, making the Fahrenheit 451 ebook available for public lending libraries (which had been against Simon & Schuster's policies at that point.)

Lesson 24

The Sci-Fi: *The Mote in God's Eye.* **Novel by Larry Niven and Jerry Pournelle**

The Sci-Fi Sitch: *Mote* tells a story of a reality that deviated from our own timeline in about 1969, when Armstrong visited the moon. In this Niven/Pournelle universe, the first successful interstellar drive was tested in 2008, and interstellar colonies established in 2020. An 'Anderson Drive' and 'Langston Field' made journeys of hundreds of light-years possible. Wars and dark ages take place, and finally, at the time in which the story of *The Mote in God's Eye* takes place, the Empire of Man rules, governed by a theocratic aristocracy. The space navy makes first contact in 3017. *Mote* is a deep, complicated tale, and a Sci-Fi milestone by a team that stands among the very best the field has to offer. But for our purposes, we'll concentrate on the prologue, which is presented as an excerpt from a speech delivered by Dr. Anthony Horvath (a character in *Mote*) at the Blaine Institute (Blaine being another character in the novel), in A.D. 3029 (twelve years after the first alien contact with the Moties, which is the subject of the novel).

"Because of the Alderson Drive we need never consider the space between the stars. Because we can shunt between stellar systems in zero time, our ships and ships' drives need cover only interplanetary distances. We say that the Second Empire of Man rules two hundred worlds and all the space between, over fifteen million cubic parsecs... Consider the true picture. Think of myriads of tiny bubbles, very sparsely scattered, rising through a vast black sea. We rule some of the bubbles. Of the waters, we know nothing..."

The Sales Sitch: Horvath's description of humanity's Empire in the year 3029 might also be an accurate representation of your sales empire, particularly if you have a large geographic area to cover. I'll use my own current situation as an example here-- my territory covers over 100,000 square miles, comprising a few population centers and the very rural land between these centers. Unless time is very short and I have no wiggle room in my schedule, I make it a point to drive, rather than fly, between the bigger towns, and to drive rather than fly whenever possible when I have sales meetings outside of my territory, in order to stop in and visit with any clients or prospects that happen to be included on the route that my drive will take me. This gives me the chance both to visit clients in the rural areas, and to prospect for new business in regions that are under-served by the competition. It puts me in touch with the people to whom I'm pitching my product, and even if I don't get in to meet with a decision maker, the very fact that I was physically in to the front desk and left, rather than mailed, a drop-off or promo material, scores me some brownie points with the prospects. While it is true that these markets are often small compared to the ones in the more urban centers, it is also true that a few small sales can add up fast to equal a large sale, and these clients are often much more loyal, because they appreciate the time and effort that you have spent to visit them on their own home grounds.

The Sales and Sci-Fi Lesson: Don't neglect the smaller markets, even if it takes a bit more effort to include them in your itinerary. You may discover more sales potential than you realized existed in the waters between the bubbles.

The Sci-Fi Skinny: Frequent collaborators Larry Niven (American writer, b. 1938) and Jerry Pournelle (American writer, b. 1933) apparently set out to write the ultimate first-contact story, and chose to set it in Pournelle's CoDominium universe. It was nominated for both the Hugo and Locus awards for 1975. Robert Heinlein said of *Mote*, "possibly the finest science fiction novel I have ever read," and Theodore Sturgeon noted it was, "one of the most engrossing tales I have encountered in years."

Lesson 25

The Sci-Fi: *Absolution Gap.* **Novel by Alastair Reynolds.**

The Sci-Fi Sitch: In a theme with an aspect similar to that in the Safehold books by David Weber, the universe of *Absolution Gap* is one in which an alien enemy exists with a mission to track and destroy any life forms or civilizations that evolve to a certain level of technology. In *Absolution Gap*, what caught my attention, however, was the story of Horris Quaiche, who joined the ship *Gnostic Ascension* as a sort of consultant to help guide the ship to exceptional financial opportunities within the various systems to which it traveled. Or, as the sado-masochistic queen and absolute ruler of the ship put it, Quaiche's task was "greasing the wheels of trade with [his] innate charm and grasp of planetary psychologies and landscapes." Much to his chagrin, however, over the course of five systems, the best that he can claim is that the ship and crew had experienced no fatalities or major injuries. When he tries to argue that he found no profit in these systems because of the simple fact that there were none to be found, the queen confronts him with the news that a different ship, visiting one of the systems right after the *Gnostic Ascension* had been there, had stumbled onto an incredibly valuable cache of trade artifacts.

It turns out that Horris Quaiche had padded his resume, as it were, when representing his skill and talent while seeking a position on the ship. In the wake of his poor performance, the queen has double-checked his background, and discovered his exaggerations of past successes. As the ship enters another system, the queen gives Quaiche one last chance to redeem himself-- she locks his girlfriend into the scrimshaw suit (a torture device), and sends him out to do his thing, with the promise that the only way to save his significant other is by succeeding in his task.

The Sales Sitch: Some great sales reps are legends in their own time. Many more are legends in their own minds. These two states of being are not mutually exclusive, nor is the latter necessarily a bad thing. Practically every really good sales rep I've ever known has had a very big, very strong ego, whether or not it showed to the general public. And it's not a sin to talk yourself or your product up to the prospects. After all, if *you* don't take pride in yourself and what you represent, why in the world would anyone pay money for your service or your product? A major part of selling is letting someone know how good you, your service and your product are. But for a lot of us, that's not the half of it. The real work comes after the sale is made, and you and your product have to live up to the hype. Some sales reps are in situations where once the sale is made, they need never have contact with the client ever again, and in these cases, some may take advantage and say whatever they have to in order to make the sale.

But there are so, so many of us who are also involved in the service after the sale, or at the very least, post-sale upsell or referral opportunities. And in these cases, if the reality of the product or service *doesn't* live up to the pre-sale promises, it's not our significant others, but ourselves, who can end up in the scrimshaw torture suits. So, yes, talk up your sales and service. Let the prospect know how great you are, and how much the product will benefit them and make their life better. But also be sure that the promises you make are realistic, because getting a bad reputation amongst prospects can lead to an existence every bit as uncomfortable as the scrimshaw suit.

The Sales and Sci-Fi Lesson: Be proud of yourself and your product, and don't hesitate to talk yourself up, but be sure that your promises can realistically be fulfilled after the sale is made.

The Sci-Fi Skinny: *Absolution Gap* is the final book in the Revelation Space trilogy by Alastair Reynolds (British writer, b. 1966) that includes *Revelation Space* and *Redemption Ark*. The first two books were selected as award-winners by both the Science Fiction Chronicle and Locus, and Absolution was named One of the Best Science Fiction Novels of the Year by Locus and One of the Top Ten Science Fiction Novels of the Year by SF Site.

Lesson 26

The Sci-Fi: *The Terminator.* **Movie, directed and co-written by James Cameron**

The Sci-Fi Stitch: A terminator cyborg has been sent from the future in a last ditch effort by the AI robots to win their war against humanity. A metal killing machine sheathed in a human body, this terminator has been sent back to the 1980s to eliminate Sarah Connor before she can give birth to her son, John, who grows up to be the leader of the human resistance that defeats the machines. John sends one of his soldiers, Kyle Reese, back to protect his mother, and he finds Sarah just in time to get her away from the Terminator, who has tracked her down after killing other women named Sarah Connor, and even *our* Sarah's roommate by mistake. The police have also noticed that someone is going around killing all the Sarah Connors he can find, and they take her and her human bodyguard, Reese, into protective custody. The Terminator shows up at the police station, goes in to the front desk, and tells the duty officer that he is there to see Sarah Connor. The policeman tells him to come back in the morning. The Terminator, looks around the room studying the space and the barricade, and then announces, in one of the most iconic lines ever uttered, "I'll be back," before he turns and leaves. A few minutes later, he drives a vehicle through the front of the building, crashing through the room, and clear through the duty desk itself. He's now in the building and begins searching for his prey, killing every policeman that gets in his way. Much chaos and carnage ensues.

The Sales Sitch: On one hand, I thought this might be a lesson on how to get past the gatekeeper. After all, who among us hasn't felt like crashing a car through the front desk when an officious secretary has totally shut us down? But in reality, the lesson here is that you may have already made the sale, you may be safely ensconced within the client's organization, and the gatekeeper may have turned a competitor's cold call away at the door. But you still never know- that Terminator might have just been scoping out the situation, assessing the weaknesses of the barriers that are keeping him or her out. And suddenly, out of nowhere, your competitor might bring a proposal crashing through the walls. It might be that your competitor develops a personal relationship with the decision-maker outside the business parameters. It might be that the competitor has spotted a flaw in your service and brings in an offer that the client can't refuse, even though you are the one on the inside, the one who has put their own body at risk for the sake of the client. Or it might just be that the competitor bulls their way past the gatekeeper and makes a presentation that blows the client away. Yes, I know how the language used to describe this scene from The Terminator is also so very applicable to the sales lesson... it's because this scene really can be an almost perfect analog or metaphor for the sales lesson. The Terminator is at the gate, and you can never, never be completely safe from an aggressive competitor.

The Sales and Sci-Fi Lesson: Even with your safest client, the competition will be looking for a way to break through with a *killer* proposal. (Hyuk, hyuk.)

The Sci-Fi Skinny: This 1984 movie was quite the Cinderella story; with no great expectations for success, either critically or commercially, *The Terminator* hit the top of the box office for two weeks, spawned three sequels, a television series, comic books, etc., and Arnold Schwarzenegger's portrayal of the assassin cyborg became one of the icons of Sci-Fi film. For James Cameron (Canadian director, producer, screen writer, b. 1954), *The Terminator* was the first major film in a growing body of work in Sci-Fi and Spec-Fic film, a stepping-stone to a monster career in mainstream film in general and Spec-Fic film in particular. *Terminator* garnered Cameron a Saturn award for Best Writing.

Lesson 27

The Sci-Fi: *Whose Face This Is I Do Not Know.* **Short story by Cat Rambo.**

The Sci-Fi Stitch: This is a short story told in the first person, that person being a laboratory experiment who has managed to escape and live on her own in the forest. As a result of the science experiment, this character is a shape-shifter, but her form changes gradually, and as we learn, to some degree in response to the desires and expectations of the people around her. She has no control over what her appearance and form will become, and is instead subject to the whims and feelings of those people in whose company she finds herself.

The Sales Sitch: As a sales rep, the title of this story sometimes captures perfectly our feelings as we look in the mirror in the mornings. Our jobs demand many roles of us, different ones depending upon our field, but always several faces that we must show to the world. These can include, of course, the hungry and high achieving salesman or saleswoman, but can also be other things; for example, to the prospect, we may need to take on the role of a problem solver or innovator, or gopher. To the client, we may be expected to be a trouble-shooter, a financial adviser, a sounding-board or confidant. Co-workers may also expect us to listen to complaints, to be a friend during times of need. The corporate brass expects us not only to sell, but to make business projections, to analyze the offerings of the competitors, to appear in public as the face of the company, and even, at times, to be a good soldier who will take a bullet for the team. Throw on top of this the roles in our lives outside of our jobs, such as spouse, parent, sibling, child, community member, PTA member, carpool driver, and so on and so on, and we, too, may take a look at ourselves and howl, "Whose face this is, I do not know!"

And there's not much that a person can do to change this; short of a major and radical life change, you won't be able to shed many, if any, of these faces, these roles that you have. But if you can keep the fact of these many roles in mind, to be aware of the many demands upon your identity, then it is easier to keep them in balance. And easier to recognize when they are becoming overwhelming, and to realize that perhaps you need to take a step back and give yourself a breather from it all.

Unlike the character in Rambo's story, we do have some control over what face we show and what role we play at any given moment. We can analyze and direct our "faces," and determine if one face is taking over too much of our life, or if another face is not getting the time it needs in order to do what needs to be done.

The Sales and Sci-Fi Lesson: The world, both professional and personal, demands that you play many different roles. Be aware of these pressures; strive to balance them, and give yourself permission to step back from them from time to time.

The Sci-Fi Skinny: Besides having one of the coolest names in all of Sci-Fi, Cat Rambo (American writer, editor, b. 1963) is a prolific author of short fiction, and teaches at Bellevue College in Washington, and via online classes. *Whose Face This Is I Do Not Know* was published in *Clarkesworld Magazine* in May, 2011. When I asked her about this story, she e-mailed the following:

> I wrote the story in part as a reaction to a workshop where a classmate said how much he hated the stories where characters were looking at themselves in mirrors or other reflective surfaces in order to let the author describe them. I started thinking about valid reasons for a character to be looking in a mirror and came up with the idea of one that literally didn't know what their appearance was at any given moment.

Ever since she told me this, I've noticed so many stories that do utilize this technique (protagonist looking at herself or himself in a reflective surface in order to provide a description for the reader), and as Cat Rambo noted, usually without any valid reason to be doing so. (I even noticed it in one of my own short stories, but I had a real and compelling reason for it. Honest!) Now that it's been pointed out, I predict that you'll notice it in your future readings as well.

Lesson 28

The Sci-Fi: *The Majipoor Chronicles.* **Short story collection by Robert Silverberg**

The Sci-Fi Sitch: *The Majipoor Chronicles* is a collection of stories from the world that is the setting of Robert Silverberg's *Lord Valentine's Castle.* The world of Majipoor sometimes reads like a fantasy, but I do classify it as science-fiction, Majipoor being a planet of enormous size, but low density, populated by various alien races, including humans, and the indigenous race of the Metamorphs. The human Coronal rules Majipoor from atop the Castle Mount, while the bulk of the administration's bureaucracy toils away beneath the planet's surface in the Labyrinth. The current Coronal, Lord Valentine, was aided in his quest to retake the crown by a clever street urchin of sorts, a denizen of the Labyrinth. Upon his return to the position of power, Valentine rewarded the youth, Hissune, with a position within the bureaucracy. Boring, boring, boring for an intelligent young teen, and his attention is drawn to the nearby offices of the Register of Souls, in which the experiences and lives of millions of people from throughout the history of Majipoor have been recorded. But how to gain entry into this restricted area? Hissune approaches the guardian on duty at the door to the Register, wondering what ruse or artifice he can use in order to gain admittance. He presents his identification, and... the gatekeeper doesn't bat an eye, but leads him in and shows him how to use the equipment.

The Sales Sitch: We've all been there, trying to figure out how in the world we can get past that dreaded gatekeeper. Tall tales, half-truths, outright lies, they all bounce around in our head, because if we can just get past that front desk, we'll *surely* be rewarded with a great sale, or at least the chance to make our pitch to a decision maker. And no doubt about it, some of these guardians seem to take a particular delight in frustrating our attempts to speak with, or even to leave a message for, the prospective client. But before expending all that energy on subterfuge and razzle-dazzle, there is one strategy that might make all that plotting and planning unnecessary... you *could* just ask.

The gatekeeper might let you right on in. Or they might check the decision-maker's schedule and ask you to make an appointment. Or they might ask you to leave some information. Or they might not. But you won't know until you try, and no matter what the response, you will be further ahead than you were. If you're successful, well then, you're successful! If not, then you have at least made an assessment of the level of resistance that you will encounter at the front gate, ranging from mild to full-blown antagonism. Information is power, and you will have added information about this prospect to your arsenal.

The Sales and Sci-Fi Lesson: In your toolbox of strategies that you use in order to get past the gate-keeper, don't overlook the simplest one of all: Just ask.

The Sci-Fi Skinny: The world of Majipoor, a creation of Robert Silverberg (American writer, b. 1935) is the site of the Majipoor series, novels and stories growing from the initial novel, *Lord Valentine's Castle*, published in 1980, a Locus award winner and Hugo award nominee for 1981. *The Majipoor Chronicles* was published in 1982, and the 10 short stories that comprise the book provided Silverberg a vehicle by which to explore and present several different slice-of-life pictures from across many, many years in the history of the world of *Lord Valentine's Castle.*

Lesson 29

The Sci-Fi: *Astounding Science Fiction,* **November 1949. Industry anecdote.**

The Sci-Fi Sitch: In 1948, a reader of the genre pulp magazine *Astounding Science Fiction* sent a letter to the publication, containing a detailed critique of the contents of the magazine from November of 1949, a year in the *future* from when the letter was written. Editor John Campbell printed the letter in the November 1948 issue with a kind of a snarky comment, but in reality, set about putting together an issue for 11/1949 to match the 'letter from the future' prophecy of Richard Hoen, the 20-year-old letter writer from Buffalo, New York. He managed to publish a magazine that was remarkably close to that described by Hoen, including the same cover artist and several of the stories described in the letter, including Robert Heinlein's *Gulf,* as well as stories by A. E. van Vogt, Lester del Rey, L. Sprague de Camp and Theodore Sturgeon.

The Sales Sitch: In the predicted issue, *Astounding Science Fiction,* November 1949, John Campbell writes in his editorial "Generally, a desirable, practically attainable idea, suggested in prophecy, has a chance of forcing itself into reality by its very existence. Like, for example, this particular issue of Astounding Science Fiction." By stating, or prophesying, a particular development or outcome, science-fiction fan Richard Hoen *actually created* that outcome. It didn't fall out of the clear blue sky; Campbell obviously had to go to a lot of effort to plan and commission the specific cover art and magazine content to make this issue happen. But the point is, it *did* happen. At the risk of sounding like Little Miss Sunshine, the lesson here is that it can be beneficial to state or predict positive outcomes for yourself. If what Campbell said has any validity, you'll be doing yourself a big favor by visualizing success. And by the same token, you'll be putting yourself at a big disadvantage if you anticipate failure in your attempts, in your projects, and in your career.

The Sales and Sci-Fi Lesson: Visualize the outcome that you want to happen, because "a desirable, practically attainable idea, suggested in prophecy, has a chance of forcing itself into reality by its very existence..."

The Sci-Fi Skinny: John Campbell, as the editor of *Astounding*, had a stable of writers included many of the names that we remember from that period, and in fact, he helped to make them memorable. This one issue of *Astounding* alone, the November 1949 issue, has Heinlein (under a pen name), Asimov, Sturgeon, van Vogt, del Rey and de Camp.

More back-story on this particular story of the letter from the future actually includes a bonus sales lesson. (Hoo-rah!) Apparently, Richard Hoen had forgotten about the letter he had written to Astounding. After all, when it was published, Campbell had included an editor's note that went something like, "Hm-m-m -- he must be off on another time-track. 'Fraid it's not THIS November '49." And then, out of the blue, nearly a year later, Campbell sent him a fully autographed copy of the Astounding that he had predicted. As *SciFi Scope* notes, "*Time* then interviewed Hoen, who said 'I'd forgotten all about my letter. They didn't even answer it.'" The lesson-- and it's related to the lesson from Ray Bradbury in *Fahrenheit 451*-- is that your comments, letters, memos, e-mails, blog posts, forum comments, *any* communications can take on a life of their own. Once you've put them out there, whether it's intended for one person or for the world, whether it's intended for a day or for eternity, once it is communicated, it is out of your control. The **bonus** Sales and Sci-Fi Lesson (Cha-ching!): Don't say, or communicate, anything ever that you aren't willing to take responsibility for at any time in the future.

Another note on the backstory of this story- the Heinlein story that was included in Astounding 11/1949 was *Gulf*, part 1 of 2, and *Gulf* was a sort of prequel to *Friday*, RAH's 1982 novel of a genetically enhanced young woman, one his more underrated later works, IMHO.

Lesson 30

The Sci-Fi: *Alien.* **Novelization by Alan Dean Foster of the movie directed by Ridley Scott.**

The Sci-Fi Sitch: The crew of the interstellar tug *Nostromo* awakens its crew from their hypersleep. The trouble is, the ship is nowhere near back to the Earth's solar system yet. Instead, the *Nostromo* had received a signal. An emergency distress signal is one of the things that will cause the ship to interrupt its pre-scheduled journey, and although this signal is confusing, the ship believes it may, in fact, be such a distress call. The signal is very alien, however, and seems to be confusing the ship's computer, and it is only an assumption that it is a call for assistance. Hence, the awakening of the crew and the detour to the desolate bit of space in which they now find themselves.

While many of the other crew are out exploring to find the nature of the emergency, Warrant Officer Ripley tinkers with the reception of the distress signal, to try and get it figured out or deciphered. When she gets the ship's computer- called 'Mother'- to work on decoding the signal some more, the computer comes to the conclusion that the transmission might *not* really be an S.O.S., but instead, a warning.

Things go downhill from there; one of the exploring crew members unknowingly gets an alien larvae implanted inside him, it bursts out of his body at the dinner table, and carnage ensues. Everyone dies except for Ripley and the ship's pet cat. (The good news, though, is that Ripley is good to go for a couple of sequels.)

The Sales Sitch: The lesson is that it is really, *really* important to have clear communications. It's actually a tad bit more complicated than this in the story, because there's the bit about the android science officer and the greed of the Company that employs the crew of the tug. But what really struck me about *Alien* as a lesson for a sales rep is that you *really* need to be sure you are reading the signals correctly that the client or prospect is sending out. If you read the signals wrong, such as misinterpreting one objection for another, then best case scenario, you'll waste time addressing a non-existent problem. Worst case scenario, you'll never get around to giving the prospect the information they need in order to buy your product. A classic misinterpretation is if the prospect is actually ready to buy, and you fail to pick up on it, and keep selling, and selling, and selling.

Once they want to buy, the more you keep talking, the more opportunity you have of putting the kibosh on the whole deal. And I'm sure you can name other situations in which a failure on your part to correctly identify the message being put out by the prospect has resulted in a lost sales opportunity. In other words, when you don't read the signals correctly, your sale can end up just as dead as the crew of the *Nostromo*.

The Sales and Sci-Fi Lesson: Correctly interpreting the signals being sent by prospects and clients is critical to your sales success.

The Sci-Fi Skinny: The 1979 movie *Alien* is billed as "The Classic Film of Ultimate Terror" and it's pretty much a scary movie, alright. (Note to grammar geeks, I'm intentionally using "alright" in this context, e-mail me if you want to debate about it…) The buggy, no-eyed, acid-bleeding alien from this story has become a science fiction icon, with sequels and prequels and crossovers and games and more. The awards garnered by this film and the people who worked on it are numerous, including an Oscar, a Hugo, awards from BAFTA and the Academy of Science Fiction, Fantasy & Horror Films, and more. It's also notable that it was directed by SF film icon Ridley Scott (and a sequel by James Cameron) and novelized in 1979 by Alan Dean Foster, who, as I've said before, is the best there is at adding depth and texture to science-fiction films by way of novelization.

And lest we neglect Sigourney Weaver, who played Ripley in *Alien*, she's also got SF chops. In addition to all the Alien-related stuff that she's done, she's also voiced roles in *WALL-E* and *Futurama*, and acted in other Spec Fic movies such as *Ghostbusters*, *Holes* (yes, *Holes* qualifies as Spec Fic), *Galaxy Quest*, and another little James Cameron film that you might have heard of, *Avatar*.

Lesson 31

The Sci-Fi: William Shatner and Leonard Nimoy. Industry anecdote.

The Sci-Fi Sitch: In 1967, the world saw a science fiction television drama hit the small screen. *Star Trek* lasted three seasons, and immediately spawned a Saturday morning cartoon spin-off, as well as books and comics and fan conventions. A decade later, a motion picture. Then more movies, syndicated sequel television series, and finally, well into the new millennium, a motion picture re-boot trilogy. Much of the enduring success of Star Trek has to be laid at the feet of William Shatner, who played the dashing self-confident Captain James T. Kirk, and Leonard Nimoy, who played the hyper-logical, faintly sinister and mysterious half-human, half-Vulcan science officer Mr. Spock.

But on the other side of the coin, perhaps much of the subsequent success of the long and profitable careers of both Shatner and Nimoy has to be laid at the feet of *Star Trek*. The franchise gave them characters that really captured peoples' imaginations, and through the following years and decades, gave them opportunities to act, write, direct and appear at conventions. Both men have done other things with their lives, big and significant projects, but the world will always know them first and foremost as Kirk and Spock.

And while the upside is obvious (more fame and fortune than you can shake a stick at), it can't have always been easy to be the focus of what many feel to be a Sci-Fi cult. You probably personally know some Trek fans who memorize the language of the Klingons or who have studied the blueprints of the *USS Enterprise* until they can watch an episode and point out a door on the set and tell you where it is supposed to lead. (Or you might even be one of these kind of fans yourself.) The fans who dress up as characters from the show, who obsess over not only the characters, but over the private lives of the people who portray those characters. The money and the acclaim that *Star Trek* brought to William Shatner and Leonard Nimoy was not without some stress and sacrifice, not without some aspects that would, understandably, bring along a small twinge of resentment.

These actors' ambivalence about their Trek roles has peeked through in the past. Take situations such as Shatner's skit on *Saturday Night Live* in which he portrays himself at a Trek convention, becoming exasperated with the fans and telling them to go out and get a real life. Or such as Nimoy's book, *I Am Not Spock,* his 1975 autobiography in which he sought to establish a distance between himself and his role. Yet, to invoke a phrase from another *SNL* skit (unrelated but very appropriate), Star Trek "been berry, berry good" to Shatner and Nimoy. Above and beyond the series and the conventions and the what-not, Shatner has written a number of science fiction novels, some set in the Trek universe. Nimoy's Spock, despite having been killed off in one of the early TOS Trek films, returned to the franchise's storyline, and even had a part in the J.J. Abrams Star Trek re-boot movie.

To be fair, I'm not saying that these two actors go around bad-mouthing Trek, or complaining about their lives. Nimoy did pen a subsequent book called *I am Spock.* And in the dedication of his novel, *Star Trek Spectre,* Shatner wrote, "Star Trek has been good to me: Fame, Fortune, Fantasy. But most of all, Friendship."

The Sales Sitch: What both Shatner and Nimoy have done is played to their strengths. William Shatner was a classically-trained Shakespearean stage actor. Leonard Nimoy is a gifted actor and photographer who made no secret of the fact that Spock gave him a bit of an identity crisis. But the Kirk and Spock characters are what they do *so well,* and they are what the audiences respond to. In Shatner's case, he's also taken the larger-than-life charisma of Kirk and translated it to other roles and personas, such as T.J. Hooker and the Priceline Negotiator. Kirk even showed up on a broadcast of the Academy Awards, with "advice from the future." And so, these actors keep coming back to these roles, these types of characters that have garnered them such success. If marketing is what you do *so well,* and it is what prospects respond to and it is what gets you sales, then keep coming back to that role. If wowing a client with the technology of your product is what your strength is, then play to it. If your strength is in providing outstanding service to your clients, then make sure your prospects know it, use testimonials from your loyal clients to make your case.

The point is, find your strength and play it to the hilt. Don't let a sales guru, an expert, or even your manager, tell you that you have to do something different. Of course, this only applies if you are being successful; just because you like a certain mode of operation doesn't mean it's your strength. It's only a strength if it is producing good results. But once you do find that strength, run with it for all it's worth.

The Sales and Sci-Fi Lesson: Discover your strengths that lead to success, and then play to them, for all you're worth.

The Sci-Fi Skinny: I have had the honor of hearing both William Shatner (Canadian actor, writer, director, b. 1931) and Leonard Nimoy (American actor, director, photographer, b. 1931) speak in person. I don't pretend to know either of them, but do hold both in the highest regard. Related **bonus** Sales and Sci-Fi Lesson: If you've been in sales any amount of time at all, you've probably run across the advice to find photos of things relating to your goals, such as a new house, or a great new car, or something to represent your child's college tuition, and stick them up on your bulletin board or somesuch. One of the things that I have posted on my board in my office isn't so much one of my goals, but is a magazine clipping intended to remind me of the lesson to play to your strengths; I don't recall what business magazine it came from, nor what year it is from, but it is a sidebar item with a photo of Shatner, noting that the Toronto Sun reported that his shares in web-based Priceline travel site were worth $582 million. That's $582,000,000. 582. Million. Dollars. ("Wait, what?") And *that's* a great reminder of what playing to your strengths can do for you.

Lesson 32

The Sci-Fi: *Perchance to Dream.* **Short story by Ariel Rodman.**

The Sci-Fi Sitch: Within the near future, technology has advanced and developed regarding sleep and dreams. "Dream centers" populate the countryside, both as public services and as private enterprises, analogous to libraries and bookstores. Directed dreaming can be a form of entertainment-- as in dreaming that one is a hero in an adventure, or a popular movie star-- or can be more purposeful-- as in using untapped potential of the human brain to make technological and scientific leaps forward. The protagonist is a school teacher who laments unproductive dreaming, and society's dismissive attitude toward more productive dreaming. As the story ends, she enters the sleep state, searching for that unknown something within her dreams that will serve to benefit humanity.

The Sales Sitch: Dreams (as in our aspirations) are what have brought a lot of us to sales, the dreams of uncapped earning potential; dreams of being rewarded for hard work, rather than being trapped in a career where people are paid for their time, regardless of talent or success, or lack of same. And it is important to keep those dreams alive and focused while the day-to-day life in the sales trenches is trying to grind us down. These dreams, the wishful thinking of our conscious hours, can also help to direct the true dreams of our sleeping hours, if we let them. Perhaps literally; I often do dream of being in a sales situation. Or perhaps figuratively; Theodore Sturgeon speaks to this sort of subconscious activity in the foreword to his collection of short stories, *Theodore Sturgeon is Alive and Well.* If nothing else, the idea of purposeful and directed dreaming helps to keep us directed toward our goals.

The Sales and Sci-Fi Lesson: Stay focused on your goals, and work through your problems, with the help of purposeful and directed "dreaming." As new age as it may sound, it *is* possible that your inner, unknown self may be able to help you to achieve your goals.

The Sci-Fi Skinny: This tale was accepted for a small online startup called *Nth Danger Spec*, as the cover story for the inaugural issue in winter 2012/2013. The author, Ariel Rodman (American writer, b. 1968), has drawn extensively from current reality for this piece and has extrapolated a future based upon the dream and sleep science and research that is taking place as of today.

As for the reference above to Theodore Sturgeon (American writer, 1918 – 1985), and allowing the dream or unconscious self to work for you — Sturgeon, as a writer, apparently had bouts of productivity… and bouts of severe unproductivity. Even though he had a few stories published in the time frame of 1940 to 1946, only one of those had been written subsequent to 1940, and he considered these years to be quite a gap in his bibliography. In the late '60s, his output was so meager that when he finally did pull a batch of short stories together (ready in 1970, published in 1971), the collection was titled, *Theodore Sturgeon is Alive and Well*, a reference to the fact that so little had been heard from him in recent history, that readers might have assumed he had shuffled off this mortal coil. Aside from one story in the collection that was written in 1954, the remaining eleven stories gathered together were all written in 1969 or 1970. Or as Sturgeon puts it, they were typed in '69 and '70, after having been written and finished in his brain. In his foreword to *Alive and Well,* he says that he has had to come to grips with the fact that what he called the period of silence "… was in no way a cessation, a stopping… the work never stopped." It just went on in the subconscious, as it were. He notes that in the time leading up to publication of the book in question, when words were not being written and pages were not being typed, that he did "other things instead, in absolute confidence that when that silent subterranean work is done, it will surface."

Lesson 33

The Sci-Fi: *Little Brother.* **Novel by Cory Doctorow**

The Sci-Fi Sitch: In San Francisco of the near future (or perhaps even of today), a terrorist attack destroys the Bay Bridge. The Department of Homeland Security uses the bombing as an excuse to put the Bay Area under a de facto martial law. The protagonist, 17-year-old computer whiz-kid Marcus, along with three gamer buddies, is taken into custody (wrong place at the wrong time...) immediately after the bombing. Following several days of over-the-line interrogation, three of them are released, while the fourth, who was severely injured in the aftermath of the attack, remains disappeared and is presumed dead.

The DHS, under the pretext of the threat of more terror attacks, begins tracking the movements and activities of the citizens, via credit card transactions, debit cards, FasTrak toll payments, etc. Some people accept this as the cost of living in a safer world. Others, like Marcus, grow angry at this treatment and the heavy-handed and unconstitutional behavior of the federal law enforcement. Marcus becomes the reluctant ringleader of a growing group of tech-savvy youths, using their skills to disrupt the surveillance by the DHS.

At one point in the story, Marcus needs to come up with a solution to a problem. As he ponders and mulls about it, something else comes to mind; the earlier failures in his life, previous humiliations that he has suffered. "Every stupid thing I'd ever said or done..." But then he turns this around... he draws on one of these humiliations to devise an answer for his current dilemma. As he notes, "There's an alternative to dwelling on your mistakes. You can learn from them."

The Sales Sitch: We all make mistakes. If we're lucky, they're small ones that can be corrected and dismissed. If we're not so lucky, they're bigger ones that can have a big impact on our work. But either way, big or small, these mistakes do give us an opportunity to see what *didn't* work in a given situation, and hopefully, to come up with something different if we're faced with the same situation in the future.

Blair Singer notes in *Sales Dogs*, that if we burn our tongue on soup, we don't stop eating soup. We learn from the mistake, and learn what didn't work. Next time, we'll wait longer, or cool it off more. We can learn from it.

Not that it's always that easy. Marcus says in *Little Brother*, "...life's embarrassments come back to haunt us even after they're long past." And they lead to memories of other failures. But there really is something to be learned from each of these embarrassments, if you can just find it, and draw on it, and turn it to your advantage next time around.

The Sales and Sci-Fi Lesson: You *will* make mistakes. When you do, you have the choice of learning from them, or letting them drag you down. (Um, btw, the point is to choose the former.)

The Sci-Fi Skinny: *Little Brother* is set in such a near future that I would almost classify it as straight fiction, rather than science fiction. And it doesn't help that I'm just not current enough on my technology to know for sure just what of the computer and internet stuff that Doctorow discusses is fact, and which is only almost-fact.

This book garnered a slew of awards, including: New York Times Notable Children's Book of 2008, Washington Post Best Kids' Books of 2008, Los Angeles Times Best Young Adult Books of 2008, Publishers Weekly Best Books of the Year for Children's Fiction, Kirkus Reviews Best of 2008, Booklist 2008 Editors' Choice: Books for Youth, School Library Journal Best Books of 2008, 2009 Indies Choice Honor Book, 2008 Nebula Award Nominee for Best Novel, 2009 Hugo Award Nominee for Best Novel, 2009 Prometheus Award for Best Novel, and 2009 John W. Campbell Memorial Award for Best SF Novel.

Beyond the obvious nod to George Orwell inherent in the title, and noted in the author's acknowledgements, I find a lot of Heinlein in this book, from the trick of putting gravel in your shoes in order to change your identifying walk, to the quote of "When in danger and in doubt, run in circles, scream and shout," to the liberal and healthy dose of author's political commentary and advocacy of civil and personal liberty.

Lesson 34

The Sci-Fi: *Star Wars, Episode I: The Phantom Menace.* **Movie, created by George Lucas.**

The Sci-Fi Sitch: Young Anakin Skywalker, enslaved along with his mother to a junk and spare parts dealer on the planet of Tatooine, dreams of entering the podraces and winning his freedom. When some stranded Jedis need some parts for their spaceship, they spot Anakin's Jedi potential, and make a wager with the junk dealer, and the boy gets his chance to race. Even though humans are considered to have inadequate reflexes for the races, his competitors apparently feel he is a real threat, because the lizard guy who is favored to win actually goes so far as to sabotage Anakin's racer.

And despite the cheating against him, despite the fact that his racer is damaged and performing at far less than its maximum potential, this future-Sith wins the race.

The Sales Sitch: The fact is, it's not the equipment, the company, or the product that is most important in a sale; it's the person. As Jeffrey Gitomer says, all things being equal, a person prefers to buy from someone they like... and even all things being *unequal*, they *still* prefer to buy from someone they like. This is why sales is as much of an art as it is a science. If sales were pure numbers, then it wouldn't even matter who was doing the selling; prospects would simply line the products up against each other and see which one scored highest on a given number of characteristics, such as price, tech support, ease of use, etc. But there is the art to selling that also comes into play. The rapport between prospect and rep, the talent on the part of the rep in presenting the features and benefits of the product, the skill of the rep in discovering the real needs of the prospect and the products to best meet those needs, the expertise in providing service after the sale. The personal touch by the rep is how products that are second-, third-, or even fourth-best can still thrive in the market. And a lack of skill on the part of the rep can be the reason that even a product that is head-and-shoulders above the competition can flounder in the market.

The Sales and Sci-Fi Lesson: Success is not so much dependent upon what is under the hood, as it is upon who is behind the wheel. People buy from people they like.

The Sci-Fi Skinny: This part of the Star Wars saga came from the 4th movie in the series, the first movie in the prequel trilogy. Anakin is the little boy who is, perhaps, the prophesied Chosen One who is incredibly gifted in the Force. But the Jedi council feels he has been discovered too late, that he is already too old to train him adequately as a Jedi. So Obi Wan takes it on himself to provide an education for him. He grows up full of anger, falls under the sway of the Sith Emperor, fathers Luke and Leia, and ultimately redeems himself by defending an adult Luke against the Emperor, dying in the process. Ah, good times.

Lesson 35

The Sci-Fi: Sturgeon's Law. Industry anecdote.

The Sci-Fi Sitch: The early days of science-fiction literature, when the genre was found mostly in the pulps and really not taken all that seriously, were a time when fans and pros interacted, when the readers wrote and the writers read. There is still much of that flavor in the genre today; look no further than the Hugos, where the cream of each year's crop is not chosen by "members of the academy" or critics, but by the *fans*. And in the era that gave birth to this give-and-take between writers and readers, it seems that so many of those pioneers in the genre contributed thoughts above and beyond their fiction. Some developed concepts that would become the very foundations (pun intended) of certain themes, such as Asimov's Laws of Robotics and the positronic brain or Heinlein's Future History. Others arrived at laws designed to help explain the universe, both fictional and non-fictional, such as Clarke's Law (found in a later *Sales and Science Fiction* lesson) and Sturgeon's Law, namely "Ninety percent of everything is crud."

The Sales Sitch: You've got a list of leads: Ninety percent of them won't even be worth your time. The marketing department develops fliers, brochures and other collateral materials- and ninety percent of the stuff doesn't accurately describe the product. The product gets delivered to the client- and ninety percent of its features are no better than, and perhaps worse than, the features on the competitor's product. But that ten percent! Oh, that golden, god-given, hallelujah-singing, bliss-inducing ten percent that makes the whole job worthwhile! The ten percent of the leads on the list that really are viable prospects that just might buy if you do a good job of selling. The ten percent of the marketing material that really captures the essence of the product in glowing, immortal prose and pix. The ten percent of your product's features that absolutely blow the competition out of the water, that represent a quantum leap in service, a leap that leaves all the other companies playing catch-up and "me, too." Sturgeon's Law is right, but it's the flip-side of that law (that he reportedly also noted, but that never gets quoted) that the remaining ten percent is *not* crud. And it's our job as sales reps to recognize and celebrate that ten percent in everything we see and do, on both the selling side and the prospect/client side of the transaction.

The Sales and Sci-Fi Lesson: Ninety percent of everything is crud. So find and cherish the ten percent that isn't. And sell the heck out of it.

The Sci-Fi Skinny: The origins of this law seem to be best and most accurately captured by James Gunn, elder statesman of the genre of science-fiction. The text here is an addendum to his review of *The Ultimate Egoist: Volume 1: The Complete Stories of Theodore Sturgeon*, which originally appeared in *The New York Review of Science Fiction #85*, September 1995, and he has graciously granted his permission for me to reproduce it here.

Sturgeon's Law was first laid down at a session of the World Science Fiction Covention in Philadelphia, held over the Labor Day weekend of 1953. It was my second convention, so it remains fresh in my memory. Many of the writers and editors that I hadn't met in Chicago, the year before, I met there: Randall Garrett, Bob Sheckley, Bob Silverberg, Harlan Ellison, Philip Jose Farmer, Ted Cogswell (who arrived on his motorcycle), all the young Turks, and some of the older ones such as Isaac Asimov, L. Sprague de Camp, and Willy Ley (whom I had at least seen in Chicago), and others whom I may have forgotten or overlooked. And Ted Sturgeon, who had brought along his 12-stringed guitar and sang Strange Fruit upon one occasion.

Of course what became known as Sturgeon's Law was then only a sentence in a talk that Ted gave to the entire convention; total membership was only 750, and there was no need for separate programming. The general thrust of Ted's remarks was that science fiction was the only genre that was evaluated by its worst examples rather than its best. "When people talk about the mystery novel," Ted said, as I remember, "they mention The Maltese Falcon and The Big Sleep. When they talk about the western, they say there's The Way West and Shane. But when they talk about science fiction, they call it 'that Buck Rogers stuff,' and they say 'ninety percent of science fiction is crud.' Well, they're right. Ninety percent of science fiction is crud. But then ninety percent of everything is crud, and it's the ten percent that isn't crud that is important. And the ten percent of science fiction that isn't crud is as good as or better than anything being written anywhere."

Lesson 36

The Sci-Fi: The Career of James Gunn. Industry anecdote.

The Sci-Fi Sitch: Speaking of James Gunn, not only is he one of the most respected authors in the field, with nearly a hundred stories published since 1948, and a new book, *Transcendental*, being published by TOR, but he is also the founding director of the Center for the Study of Science Fiction at Kansas University, and the author of several books about the field and craft of science fiction writing, including *The Science of Science-Fiction Writing*. Not only is he an acknowledged expert *in* the field of science fiction (a Grand Master, in fact), but he is an acknowledged expert *on* the field of science fiction.

The Sales Sitch: Many of us are familiar with the phrase from academia, "Publish or perish," but for a sales professional, it might better be interpreted as "Publish to promote." And after that, "Promote or perish." It is easier for a client or prospect to place trust and confidence in what their sales rep tells them if that sales rep is also an acknowledged, published professional about whatever product or service he or she is representing. There is a mystique about being a published author, just as there is in being a journalist or an actor or in having earned your doctorate. You might know everything there is to know about your industry and no one cares, but you might know a fair amount *and* have published a book or a white paper about it, and then everyone is impressed. This is the reason that you might see a column regarding real estate issues or legal issues or something similar in your local newspaper, written by a local Realtor or lawyer. They get the double bonus of getting their name out in front of the general public on a regular basis, plus they get the added benefit of having the cachet of being a "published expert" on the subject. So if you are in the position of having published *anything* within your field, then play this up, make sure all your prospects know it, and milk it for all it is worth.

The Sales and Sci-Fi Lesson: Being a published author gives you an aura of professionalism and expertise that you can leverage into sales clout.

The Sci-Fi Skinny: James Gunn (American writer, editor, b. 1923), as noted, is not only one of the authors who pioneered the field of science fiction, but *continues* to be a pioneer, with the Center for the Study of Science Fiction at KU, his online journal of fiction and non-fiction *Ad Astra*, and a new novel. And while I was researching this book, he was very candid with me and noted that he found that being a scholar *of* science fiction (that is, a published author *about* the genre) was *not* of particular benefit in selling his science-fiction stories. The mystique of writing, or acting, doesn't have as much impact *in* the fields of writing, or of acting. Instead, publishers or producers are more interested in past performance as an indicator of future performance. For more on this, see *Sales and Science Fiction* Lesson #41.

Lesson 37

The Sci-Fi: *Bicentennial Man.* **Novelette by Isaac Asimov.**

The Sci-Fi Sitch: In this Asimov novelette, a household robot, tasked with taking care of the children, gradually comes to exhibit an artistic talent. Encouraged by his human owners, the robot pursues its interest, and even finds it to be "enjoyable." He becomes known as Andrew Martin, in order to have a bank account and keep earnings from his artistic endeavors, and seems to be a true AI, Artificial Intelligence, a vindication of the Descartes statement, "I think, therefore I am." As the years go by, he becomes more physically human in appearance, trading in and upgrading his robot body for an android body, and comes closer and closer to gaining legal standing as a human. He finally succeeds in having his positronic brain altered so that it will decay, like a biological human brain, and achieves true "humanity"– and mortality- passing away at age 200, hence the title of the work.

The Sales Sitch: As a species, we humans have a love-hate relationship with machines. We love how they make our lives easier, and we hate how they will one day revolt and kill us all. And in the meantime, we hate how impersonal our interactions with them can be. And as hard as it may be to believe at times, your prospects and clients *are* human. So they may love some of the great labor-saving aspects that the machines and computers involved with your product bring to their lives, they also hate dealing with those machines and computers. They want a real, live human to help them out when they encounter problems. Don't believe me? Try calling your long-distance telephone provider with a question and see if you're satisfied with the robot customer service.

Even Asimov's Andrew Martin preferred human over robot; he traded a virtual immortality as a positronically-brained robot in order to be a mortal human being. So put a human face on your product and your service. Give your client a phone number that will take them to a human being. Show your human face as much as possible. Ask about their human interests and concerns, and don't be afraid to talk to them about your own human family and life.

The Sales and Sci-Fi Lesson: Put a human face on your sales and service. People don't build a rapport with an automaton.

The Sci-Fi Skinny: The Bicentennial Man is a novelette by Isaac Asimov in his Robots universe. It earned him the Hugo and the Nebula awards for Best Novelette in 1976. This story was the basis for the later novel called *The Positronic Man* in 1993, co-written by Robert Silverberg, and was adapted into a movie called *Bicentennial Man* in 1999, with Robin Williams (American comedian, actor, b. 1951) in the title role of Andrew Martin.

Lesson 38

The Sci-Fi: *The Vor Game.* **Novel by Lois Bujold McMasters.**

The Sci-Fi Sitch: Our hero, Miles Vorkosigan, is an undercover agent for his planet's Imperial Security, in a future of planetary empires, espionage, warfare and trade. In his undercover role, he is portraying Victor Rotha, Procurement Agent. And what he is supposedly procuring is illicit arms and weaponry. Miles' cover is, as he himself notes, that of a traveling salesman of death. Miles has a meeting and a sales pitch with a prospect, Mr. Liga, who shows interest, and wants to okay the purchase with his own superior. Another meeting with the prospect is set up, but when Miles gets there, he finds a different person, Livia Nu, at the agreed location. Miles asks if the newcomer is the Liga's supervisor, and she kind of goes along with that. So Miles kind of goes along with her going along. Turns out, though, that she is Liga's supervisor, only if by supervisor, you mean the person who killed him and then framed Miles for the murder.

The Sales Sitch: Miles can probably be forgiven for his blunder — he is working within several layers of espionage and deception, trying to get a lead on illegal arms deals — but he does make a classic mistake of sales, in not determining where the sales buck stops, who the decision-maker is. His sales pitch works on the first level decider, Mr. Liga, and gets him on to the next stage. But then he wastes his next pitch on someone who *wouldn't* make a purchase, and *couldn't* make a purchase, even if she wanted to. (She was too busy setting him up to take the fall for the Liga murder.) If Miles had closed his first meeting, his successful meeting, as he should have, by establishing the next steps needed to progress the sale, he would have known that the meeting with Livia Nu was *not* part of the program, and might have handled things differently.

The Sales and Sci-Fi Lesson: Don't blunder your way up the chain of command; establish from the beginning who the decision-maker is, and close each sales meeting by agreeing upon the next steps with the prospect.

The Sci-Fi Skinny: *The Vor Game* is a part of the Vorkosigan Saga by Lois Bujold McMasters (American writer, b. 1949). It was published in 1990, and earned the Hugo for Best Novel in 1991. McMasters is a very accomplished contemporary science-fiction writer, with scads of awards (Hugo, Nebula, Locus and more) and nominations to her credit.

Lesson 39

The Sci-Fi: Clarke's Third Law. Industry anecdote.

The Sci-Fi Sitch: Arthur Clarke postulated thee laws, the third of which
is: Any sufficiently advanced technology is indistinguishable from magic.

The Sales Sitch: You've met the guy or gal. The one who has to know
exactly *why* and *how* everything works, or thinks they have to know it, in
order to sell the product or service. Say you're selling encyclopedias; this
fellow in the sales force thinks he has to know *how* the publisher gathered
the knowledge that is included in the book. Or this lady in the sales force
feels that she has to know if it's printed on a lithographic press or if it
utilizes digital printing technologies.

But let me clue you in: You only need to know something if it's something
that will really help you sell the product. Is it a feature that leads to a
benefit? Or is it an interesting, but ultimately useless, bit of trivia?

Your potential encyclopedia client *probably* doesn't really care if the
polycarbonate synthetic glue that binds the cover to the pages is made
from a carbon-derivative process or from a monoethylene process. What is
probably important to the client is whether the cover is going to stay bound
to the pages. Is this accomplished by technology? Or by magic? *It doesn't
matter.* If they don't care, then you don't need to know. Sir Arthur Conan
Doyle, in the person of Dr. Watson, tells us that Sherlock Holmes, one of
the brightest guys in (fictional) history, didn't know bupkis about anything
that he didn't *need* to know about, because it didn't have any impact on the
stuff he needed to know and he didn't want to clutter up his mind with
non-essential information. As Watson notes in *A Study in Scarlet,*

> His ignorance was as remarkable as his knowledge. Of
> contemporary literature, philosophy and politics he appeared to
> know next to nothing. ... My surprise reached a climax, however,
> when I found incidentally that he was ignorant of the Copernican
> Theory and of the composition of the Solar System. That any
> civilized human being in this nineteenth century should not be
> aware that the earth travelled round the sun appeared to me to be
> such an extraordinary fact that I could hardly realize it...
>   "You see," he explained, "I consider that a man's brain originally
> is like a little empty attic, and you have to stock it with such

furniture as you choose. A fool takes in all the lumber of every sort that he comes across, so that the knowledge which might be useful to him gets crowded ... Now the skilful workman is very careful indeed as to what he takes into his brain-attic. He will have nothing but the tools which may help him in doing his work, but of these he has a large assortment, and all in the most perfect order... Depend upon it there comes a time when for every addition of knowledge you forget something that you knew before. It is of the highest importance, therefore, not to have useless facts elbowing out the useful ones."

"But the Solar System!" I protested.

"What the deuce is it to me?" he interrupted impatiently: "you say that we go round the sun. If we went round the moon it would not make a pennyworth of difference to me or to my work."

The same goes for you as a sales rep; unless it's information you need to know to; a) inform; or b) dazzle and convince your client/prospect, it's non-essential. Tech, magic, or whatever, it *doesn't matter* as long as it gets the job done.

Sales and Sci-Fi Lesson: Clarkes' Third Law, adapted to sales: Any technology that is sufficiently advanced beyond what you need to know might as well be magic, for all you know or care.

The Sci-Fi Skinny: Arthur C. Clarke postulated the following three laws:
- When a distinguished but elderly scientist states that something is possible, he is almost certainly right. When he states that something is impossible, he is very probably wrong.
- The only way of discovering the limits of the possible is to venture a little way past them into the impossible.
- Any sufficiently advanced technology is indistinguishable from magic.

Of the three, the third is most often cited in the world at large, and it's quoted *like crazy* within the SF genre, all the way from early (and contemporary) Doctor Who to Star Trek TNG to Girl Genius. If you didn't know Clarke's Third Law previously, I'll bet that now that it's been pointed out to you, you'll run across it in some sort of popular culture within the next week or so. Yes, it's that prevalent; almost as if it's... *magic.* ("Oooooooo-ooooooooh," he wailed, in a comic-book ghost voice.)

40: The Sci-Fi: *Blade Runner.* **Movie directed by Ridley Scott.**

The Sci-Fi Sitch: *Blade Runner* is a 1982 neo-noir film loosely based on Philip K. Dick's *Do Androids Dream of Electric Sheep?* and was directed by Ridley Scott. Harrison Ford plays a special type of cop, one who specializes in hunting down rogue 'replicants,' organic androids virtually indistinguishable from real human beings, replicants who are attempting to escape their existence as slaves and to blend in with the human population.

Following a disappointing box-office opening, and after some other behind-the-scenes industry wrangling, Warner Brothers released a director's cut version of the film, approved by Ridley Scott, in 1991. This director's cut gets rid of the voice-over narration by Ford's character, pays more attention to the romantic storyline, gets rid of the feel-good ending, and adds a certain unicorn element that is one of the linchpins for the argument that Ford's character is, in reality, a replicant himself. In other words, a very different movie, and for the most part, a much better one. (Although I have to admit, I kind of enjoyed the Harrison Ford voiceover on the original.)

The Sales Sitch: There's a lot more drama behind the scenes of this story, including an eventual "Final Cut" version released for the film's 25th anniversary, said to be the first version on which Ridley had full artistic control. But for purposes of this lesson, the point is that there were two ways to do this film, which we'll call the producer's Theatrical Version and Ridley's Director's Cut. And the Director's Cut was pretty much the superior way. Warner Brothers worded it: "The result is a heightened emotional impact: a great film made greater." And the lesson is that you have to trust the judgment of your personnel in the trenches. Ridley Scott apparently had a vision for this film that was shelved in favor of the producers' vision, but when both were put out there for evaluation by the viewers, it was Scott's version that people preferred. In other words, *Blade Runner* would have been better served by letting the professional do his job, and not trying to micro-manage him.

Likewise, you need to let your professionals do their jobs (and you need to be left to do yours.) Trust in your marketing department to know how best to get the message out to prospects. Trust in your manager to know how best to gather and implement the company's resources to your benefit. Trust in your customer service department to know best how to address a client's problems. And if you can't trust the professionals on your team to do their jobs, then you really need to try to implement some changes; changes in the people who hold those positions, or a change in your own company affiliation. And likewise, as a professional, you should be given the courtesy by those around you of being left to best do your own job.

The Sales and Sci-Fi Lesson: Trust in the professionals on your team to do their jobs competently. If they can't, some change is called for; your own job is hard enough without your having to do someone else's for them as well.

The Sci-Fi Skinny: Ridley Scott (British director, producer, b. 1937) calls *Blade Runner* his most complete and personal film. It earned him a nomination for a Saturn award for Best Director, and the film itself, among its many wins and nominations, took the Hugo award in 1983 for Best Dramatic Presentation.

Lesson 41

The Sci-Fi: *The Science of Science-Fiction Writing.* Non-fiction book by James Gunn.

The Sci-Fi Sitch: James Gunn is noted elsewhere in this book, both for the information that he provides about some of the personalities of the field, as well as for his own contributions to the genre. His non-fiction book *The Science of Science-Fiction Writing* is something that he calls "forty years of reflections about the fiction writing process and how to teach it, and the ideas I have shared with my students about how to do it effectively and how to get it published afterward." And since the job of getting published is, in essence, the job of selling-- selling one's work to a publisher, selling one's story to a reader-- some of the info in his book is directly and specifically applicable to any sales rep.

The Sales Sitch: In particular, *Chapter 4: The Author's Strategy,* and a line from *Chapter 11: How to be a Good Critiquer and Still Remain Friends* speak most directly to the sales field.

In *The Author's Strategy,* Gunn describes the strategy by which an editor makes it through the day. Given the amount of work piled onto an editor, and the glut of submissions from writers hoping to sell their work to the publisher, the editor's strategy is to weed out the proposals as quickly and cleanly as possible, trusting the cream to rise to the top, the nuggets of gold to settle to the bottom, or whatever other metaphor you prefer. The editor's strategy is to find whatever excuse to reject a proposal, so that she or he can then focus attention on whatever is left. In other words, a submission could be the literary equivalent of Shakespeare, but if it was submitted handwritten in crayon on construction paper, it probably would not stand a chance of being published. And your product might be the perfect fit or solution for a prospect, but if you misspell the name of their company on the cover sheet, or if you show up two hours late for your appointment, you can pretty much count on being winnowed out of the running for that sale.

In *How to be a Good Critiquer,* Gunn states that "The only meaningful success for a story is publication..." and that goes for sales, as well. There's no payment or royalties on a story that *almost* got published, and there's no commission check on a sale that you *almost* made.

The Sales and Sci-Fi Lesson(s):
To paraphrase James Gunn, the strategy of the sales rep must be: Don't give the prospect an excuse to say "no."

Again to paraphrase James Gunn, the only meaningful success for an interaction with a prospect is a sale (either immediately or eventually).

The Sci-Fi Skinny: James Gunn is an accomplished writer in the field of science-fiction, with novels including *The Immortals, The Joy Makers, The Listeners* and *the Dreamers,* and his published short stories number somewhere near 100. He is also an accomplished writer about the field of science-fiction, including the six-volume *The Road to Science Fiction.* Gunn has served as the president of the Science Fiction Writers of America, and as the president of the Science Fiction Research Association, and in 2007, was named a Damon Knight Memorial Grand Master. In addition to a boatload of other awards and accomplishments, Gunn is the founding director of the Center for the Study of Science Fiction at the University of Kansas.

Lesson 42

The Sci-Fi: *The Hitchhiker's Guide to the Galaxy.* **Novel by Douglas Adams.**

The Sci-Fi Sitch: In this classic British Sci-Fi farce, the Earth is destroyed in order to make way for some sort of cosmic bypass, and the only surviving Earthlings are everyman Arthur Dent, the intelligent and attractive Tricia McMillan aka Trillian, some dolphins and a pair of mice.

But wait- the mice are actually just the avatars of a pair of extradimensional beings. And the Earth wasn't just a planet, but instead, a planet-sized computer program commissioned by the mice in order to determine the Ultimate Question to Life, the Universe, and Everything. (They already had the Answer to Life, the Universe and Everything... it's 42. Now they needed the Question, in order to make sense of the Answer.) And the Earth's destruction came just before the completion of the program that would give the mice this Ultimate Question. Soooo. They can't go back to their constituents without the solution (they've been waiting some 10 million years to get this Question that will make sense of the Answer of 42). Since they don't have the real answer from the computer program, and can't re-run the program, and can't go back empty-handed, they end up brainstorming an... um... "alternate"... (that is to say, *fake*) Question to the Answer of 42. They settle on "How many roads must a man walk down?" and take this back as the solution millions of years in the making. One of the mice says, "Yes, that's excellent! Sounds very significant without actually tying you down to meaning anything at all."

The Sales Sitch: The sales situation is obvious; you have to be wary when someone- prospects, clients, or really, *anyone* at all- gives you an answer that is vague and noncommittal, an answer that doesn't tie them down to meaning anything at all. And the more important the issue is, the more highly-anticipated the answer is, the more important it is that the answer be very clear and definite.

For examples:

Q: "What is your budget for this project?"
Bad A: "Management is committed to devoting an adequate amount of resources to the project."

Good A: "Mangement is committed to devoting an adequate amount of resources to the project- we are looking for a solution in the range of $20,000 - $25,000."

Q: "What is your timeframe for this project?"
Bad A: "Once we get all the information in, we'll probably start right after that."
Good A: "Once we get all the information in, we want to get this started at the beginning of next quarter, so we'll need to have all of the preliminary groundwork done by then."

Q: "Thank you for your time. I'll take your specifications and develop a comprehensive proposal. When is the best time for me to come back and go over the proposal with you?"
Bad A: "This time of year is really hectic. Let me get back to you on that."
Good A: "This time of year is really hectic. Let's nail down a time slot next Wednesday at 9 a.m."

The Sales and Sci-Fi Lesson: Vague answers are worded that way for a reason. Strive for clear communication and answers that establish definite details, answers that are not open to misinterpretation or deliberate misdirection.

The Sci-Fi Skinny: *Hitchhiker's Guide* is a British farce in the tradition of Monty Python (Douglas Adams was a writer for the sketch comedy show), with incredibly clever and witty writing and concepts. It started out as a radio play, gained fame as a novel, and has many incarnations in many different media. The books grew to be a trilogy of some six books or so. (No, I'm not stupid, I know a trilogy is three, and so does Adams, which is why one of my copies of *Hitchhikers's Guide* has the description on the cover, "The first in the increasingly inaccurately named Hitchhiker's Trilogy.") Douglas Adams (British writer, 1952 – 2001), in addition to writing the Hitchhiker's Guide books (with the exception of the sixth, which was written by Eoin Colfer after Adams' death in 2001), had some other Spec-Fic books, such as *Dirk Gently's Holistic Detective Agency* and *The Long Dark Tea-Time of the Soul,* and wrote some Doctor Who storylines during the Tom Baker era.

Additionally, *Hitchhiker's Guide* imbues the number 42 with a mythic and iconic quality in the world of SF, making it the perfect number of lessons to include in this book. Hot-cha-cha!

Index

Numbers
2001: A Space Odyssey: Lessons 6, 10, 17
20,000 Leagues Under the Sea: Intro

A
J. J. Abrams: Lessons 12, 13, 31
Absolution Gap: Lesson 25
The Academy Awards: Lesson 6, 17, 30
The Academy of Science Fiction Fantasy & Horror Films: Lesson 30
Ace Books: Lesson 20
Douglas Adams: Lesson 42
Ad Astra: Lesson 36
Alien: Lesson 30
American Graffiti: Lesson 9
Kevin J. Anderson: Lesson 1
Angel: Lesson 18
Piers Anthony: Lesson 20
Isaac Asimov: Lessons 20, 21, 35, 37
Astounding Science-Fiction: Lessons 7, 14, 29
Avatar: Lesson 30
The Avengers: Lesson 18

B
Baen Books: Lesson 22
BAFTA: Lesson 30
Tom Baker: Lesson 42
Christian Bale: Lesson 17
BBC: Lesson 2
The Better Part of Valor: Lesson 16
The Bicentennial Man: Lesson 37
The Big Sleep: Lesson 35
Blade Runner: Lessons 17, 40
Book List: Lesson 33
Pierre Boulle: Lesson 6
Ray Bradbury: Lesson 23, 29
Buffy the Vampire Slayer: Lesson 18
Edgar Rice Burroughs: Lesson 20

C
James Cameron: Lessons 26, 30
John W. Campbell: Lessons 21, 29
Center for the Study of Science Fiction: Lessons 25, 36
Arthur C. Clarke: Lessons 10, 20, 21, 35, 39
Clarkesworld Magazine: Lesson 27
Cloud Atlas: Lesson 19
Theodore Cogswell: Lesson 35
Eoin Colfer: Lesson 42
A Confederation of Valor: Lesson 16

D
Damon Knight Memorial Grand Master: Lessons 36, 41
The Day the Earth Stood Still: Lesson 19
L. Sprague de Camp: Lessons 20, 29, 35
Lester Del Rey: Lesson 29
Del Rey Books: Lesson 20
Philip K. Dick: Lesson 20, 40
Dirk Gently's Holistic Detective Agency: Lesson 42
Disney: Intro, Lesson 9
Cory Doctorow: Lesson 33
Doctor Who: Lessons 2, 39, 42
Arthur Conan Doyle: Lesson 39
The Dreamers: Lesson 41
Dr. Horrible's Sing-Along Blog: Lesson 18
Dune: Intro, Lesson 1

E
Harlan Ellison: Lessons 20, 35

F
Philip Jose Farmer: Lessons 20, 35
Firefly: Lesson 18
Kaja Foglio: Lesson 3
Phil Foglio: Lesson 3
Harrison Ford: Lesson 40
Alan Dean Foster: Lessons 13, 20, 30
Futurama : Lesson 30
Benjamin Franklin: Lesson 21
Friday: Lesson 29

Fringe: Lesson 12

G
Galaxy Quest: Lesson 30
Randall Garrett: Lesson 35
Ghostbusters: Lesson 30
Girl Genius: Lessons 3, 39
Jeffrey Gitomer: Lesson 37
Joseph Gordon-Levitt: Lesson 17
Guardian Newspaper: Lesson 2
Guinness World Records: Lesson 2
Gulf: Lesson 29
James Gunn: Intro, Lessons 35, 36, 41

H
Have You Heard the One?: Lesson 4
Robert Heinlein: Lessons 4, 7, 11, 14, 20, 21, 24, 29, 33, 35
Virginia Heinlein: Lesson 14
Brian Herbert: Lesson 1
Frank Herbert: Intro, Lesson 1
Charlton Heston: Lesson 6
The Hitchhiker's Guide to the Galaxy: Intro, Lesson 42
Richard Hoen: Lesson 29
James P. Hogan: Lesson 20
Holes: Lesson 30
Tanya Huff: Lesson 16
Hugo Award: Lessons 1, 3, 20, 26, 28, 30, 33, 35, 37, 40
Kim Hunter: Lesson 6
Nick Hurran: Lesson 2

I
I Am Spock and *I Am Not Spock*: Lesson 34
"If This Goes On---": Lesson 7
If Magazine: Lesson 15
The Illustrated Man: Lesson 23
The Immortals: Lesson 41
Inception: Lesson 17
Indies Choice: Lesson 33
The Invisible Man: Lesson 8

J
Hugh Jackman: Lesson 17
Amy E. Boyle Jonhston: Lesson 23
Johnny Mnemonic: Lesson 19
John W. Campbell Memorial Award: Lesson 33
Robert Jordan: Lesson 20
The Joy Makers: Lesson 41

K
Stephen King: Intro, Lesson 20
Kirkus Reviews: Lesson 33
Damon Knight: Lesson 7
Stanley Kubrick: Lessons 10, 17
Alex Kurtzman: Lesson 12

L
Keith Laumer: Lessons 15, 22
Willy Ley: Lesson 35
Life-Line: Lesson 14
The Listeners: Lesson 41
Little Brother: Lesson 33
Locus Award: Lessons 24, 25, 28, 38
The Long Dark Tea-Time of the Soul: Lesson 42
Lord Valentine's Castle: Lesson 28
Los Angeles Times: Lesson 36
Lost: Lesson 12
George Lucas: Lessons 9, 34

M
The Majipoor Chronicles: Lesson 28
The Maltese Falcon: Lesson 35
The Man Who Sold the Moon: Lesson 11
The Martian Chronicles: Lesson 23
Marvel Comics: Lesson 20
The Matrix: Lesson 19
Anne McCaffrey: Lesson 20
Roddy McDowall: Lesson 6
Lois Bujold McMasters: Lesson 38
Steven Moffat: Lesson 2

Monty Python: Lesson 42
Moses: Lesson 11
The Mote in God's Eye: Lesson 24

N
Nebula Award: Lessons 1, 33, 37, 38
The New York Review of Science Fiction: Lesson 35
New York Times: Lesson 33
Nightfall: Lesson 21
Leonard Nimoy: Lesson 31
Larry Niven: Lessons 20, 24
Christopher Nolan: Lessons 17, 18
Nth Danger Spec: Lesson 32

O
Off Armageddon Reef: Lesson 22
Roberto Orci: Lesson 12
George Orwell: Lesson 33

P
The Past Through Tomorrow: Lessons 7, 11
Perchance to Dream: Lesson 32
The Philosopher at the End of the Universe: Lessons 8, 9
A Plague of Demons: Lesson 15
La Planete des singes: Lesson 6
Planet of the Apes: Lesson 6
Plato: Lesson 8
Frederik Pohl: Lesson 20
The Positronic Man: Lesson 37
Jerry Pournelle: Lessons 20, 24
The Prestige: Lesson 17
Prometheus Award: Lesson 33
Publishers Weekly: Lesson 33
Pulitzer Prize: Lesson 23

R
Cat Rambo: Lesson 27
Redemption Ark: Lesson 25
Keanu Reeves: Lesson 19
Requiem: Lesson 11

Revelation Space: Lesson 25
Revolt in 2100: Lesson 7
Alastair Reynolds: Lesson 25
The Ring of Gyges: Lesson 8
The Road to Science Fiction: Lesson 41
Spider Robinson: Lesson 4
Gene Roddenberry: Lesson 12
Ariel Rodman: Lesson 32
Mark Rowlands: Lesson 8, 9

S
Sales Dogs: Lessons 4, 33
Saturday Night Live: Lesson 31
Saturn Award: Lessons 19, 26, 40
A Scanner Darkly: Lesson 19
Franklin J. Schaffner: Lesson 6
School Library Journal: Lesson 33
Arnold Schwarzenegger: Lesson 26
Science Fiction Hall of Fame: Lesson 20
Science Fiction Chronicle: Lesson 25
Science Fiction Research Association: Lesson 41
Science Fiction Writers of America: Lessons 20, 21, 41
The Science of Science-Fiction Writing: Lessons 36, 41
SciFi Scope: Lesson 29
Ridley Scott: Lessons 17, 30, 40
The Sentinel: Lesson 10
Serenity: Lesson 18
Rod Serling: Lesson 6
SF Site: Lesson 25
William Shakespeare: Lessons 21, 41
Shane: Lesson 35
William Shatner: Lesson 31
Robert Sheckley: Lesson 35
Robert Silverberg: Lessons 28, 35, 37
Blair Singer: Lessons 4, 33
Simon & Schuster: Lesson 23
Matt Smith: Lesson 2
Solstice Award: Lesson 20
Speedracer: Lesson 19
Starship Troopers: Lesson 9

Star Trek: Lessons 12, 13, 20, 31, 39
Star Wars: Lessons 9, 12, 34
A Study in Scarlet, Lesson 39
Theodore Sturgeon: Lessons 20, 24, 29, 32, 35
Darrell K. Sweet: Lesson 20
SyFy Channel: Lesson 1

T
The Terminator: Lesson 26
Theodore Sturgeon is Alive and Well: Lesson 32
Thrilling Wonder Stories: Lesson 14
Time for the Stars: Lesson 20
Time Travelers Strictly Cash: Lesson 4
Top Science Fiction Movies: Lesson 12
TOR Books: Lessons 3, 20, 22, 36
Toronto Sun: Lesson 34
Transcendental: Lesson 36
Traveling Salesman: Lessons 4, 7
Tunnel in the Sky: Lesson 20
The Twilight Zone: Lesson 6

U
The Ultimate Egoist: Volume 1: The Complete Stories of Theodore Sturgeon:
Lesson 35

V
V for Vendetta: Lesson 19
Boris Vallejo: Lesson 20
Valor's Choice: Lesson 16
A. E. Van Vogt: Lesson 29
Variable Star: Lesson 4
Jules Verne: Intro
"--*Vine and Fig Tree*--": Lesson 7
The Vor Game: Lesson 38

W
WALL-E: Lesson 30
Warner Brothers: Lesson 40
Warner Books: Lesson 15
War of the Worlds: Lesson 5
Washington Post: Lesson 33

The Way West: Lesson 35
The Wachowskis: Lesson 19
David Weber: Lessons 22, 25
Orson Welles: Lesson 5
H. G. Wells: Lesson 5, 8
Joss Whedon: Lesson 18
Michael Whelan: Lesson 20
Whose Face This Is I Do Not Know: Lesson 27
Robin Williams: Lesson 37
Michael Wilson: Lesson 6
World Science Fiction Convention: Lessons 20, 35
Wreck-It Ralph: Lesson 9

Z

Roger Zelazny: Lesson 20

Further Info

2001: A Space Odyssey: kubrickfilms.warnerbros.com

Academy Awards: Oscar.go.com

Academy of Science Fiction Fantasy & Horror films:
www.saturnawards.org

Ace Books:
www.uspenguingroup.com/pages/publishers/adult/ace.html

Douglas Adams: www.douglasadams.com

Ad Astra: adastra.ku.edu

Kevin J. Anderson: www.wordfire.com

Isaac Asimov: www.asimoveonline.com

Baen Books: www.baen.com

BAFTA: www.bafta.org

Blade Runner: bladerunnerthemovie.warnerbros.com

Ray Bradbury: www.raybradbury.com

Center for the Study of Science Fiction: www.sfcenter.ku.edu

Arthur C. Clarke: www.arthurcclarke.net

Clarkesworld Magazine: clarkesworldmagazine.com

Damon Knight Memorial Grand Master: www.sfwa.org

Del Rey Books: sf-fantasy.suvudu.com

Philip K. Dick: www.philipkdickfans.com

Cory Doctorow: craphound.com

Doctor Who: www.bbc.co.uk/programmes/b006q2x0

Firefly: www.fireflyfans.net

Alan Dean Foster: www.alandeanfoster.com

Girl Genius: www.girlgeniusonline.com, www.studiofoglio.com

Jeffrey Gitomer: www.gitomer.com

James Gunn: www.sfcenter.ku.edu/bio.htm

Robert Heinlein: www.heinleinsociety.org

Frank Herbert: www.frankherbert.net, www.dunenovels.com

Tanya Huff: twitter.com/TanyaHuff

Hugo Award: www.thehugoawards.org

Inception: inceptionmovie.warnerbros.com/dvd

John W. Campbell Memorial Award:
www.sfcenter.ku.edu/Campbell.htm

Stanley Kubrick: kubrickfilms.warnerbros.com

Locus Award: www.locusmag.com

George Lucas: www.lucasfilm.com

Lois Bujold McMasters: www.dendarii.com

Nebula Award: www.sfwa.org

The New York Review of Science Fiction: www.nyrsf.com

Leonard Nimoy: www.theofficialleonardnimoyfanclub.com

Larry Niven: www.larryniven.net

Nth Danger Spec: www.nthdangerspec.weebly.com

Frederik Pohl: www.frederikpohl.com

Jerry Pournelle: www.jerrypournelle.com

Prometheus Award: www.lfs.org/awards.htm

Pulitzer Prize: www.pulitzer.org

Cat Rambo: www.kittywumpus.net

Alistair Reynolds: voxish.tripod.com

Spider Robinson: www.spiderrobinson.com

Ariel Rodman: www.arielrodman.weebly.com

Mark Rowlands: rowlands.philospot.com

Saturn Award: www.saturnawards.org

Science Fiction Research Association: www.sfra.org

Science Fiction Writers of America: www.sfwa.org

William Shatner: williamshatner.com

Robert Silverberg: www.majipoor.com

Blair Singer: www.blairsinger.com

Simon & Schuster: www.simonandschuster.com

Solstice Award: www.sfwa.org

Star Trek: www.startrek.com

Star Wars: starwars.com

Theodore Sturgeon: www.theodoresturgeontrust.com

Darrell K. Sweet: darrellksweet.wix.com/darrellksweet

Tor Books: www.tor.com

Boris Vallejo: www.imaginistix.com

Warner Brothers: www.warnerbros.com

Warner Books: ww.hachettebookgroup.com

David Weber: www.davidweber.net

Michael Whelan: www.michaelwhelan.com

World Science Fiction Convention: www.worldcon.org

About the author

Raymond "R. Keith" Rugg lives with his family in the Galena foothills between Lake Tahoe and Reno, Nevada. He holds a B.A. in political science, and in addition to sales, he has enjoyed success as a journalist and educator. He enjoys selling, reading, writing, running, and exploring indigenous and Native American speculative fiction.

Rugg's Handbook of Sales and Science Fiction is his first book, and is also the first of a trio of handbooks of sales and speculative fiction, to be followed by *Sales and Swords & Sorcery* and *Sales and the Supernatural*.

Like what you've seen?

Visit the website at

www.salesandscifi.weebly.com

for tips, tricks, lessons, updates, discussions and more!

And don't miss

Rugg's Handbook of Sales and Swords & Sorcery (and all sorts of Fantasy!)

Coming to print and e-book in early 2021!

www.ingramcontent.com/pod-product-compliance
Lightning Source LLC
Chambersburg PA
CBHW051546170526
45165CB00002B/899